COVID-19 PANDEMIC:

The Outbreak That Shook The World

© **Copyright 2021 - All rights reserved.**

All rights reserved. No part of this guide may be reproduced, transmitted, or distributed in any form or by any means without permission in writing from the publisher except in the case of brief quotations embodied in critical articles or reviews.

Legal & Disclaimer

The content and information in this book is consistent and truthful, and it has been provided for informational, educational and business purposes only.

The content and information contained in this book has been compiled from reliable sources, which are accurate based on the knowledge, belief, expertise and information of the Author. The author cannot be held liable for any omissions and/or errors.

Table of Contents

CHAPTER 1 5
HOW THE BIG PLAYERS COPED, CHINA, USA & INDIA. THE LOSERS & WINNERS, THE ROAD FORWARD FOR NEW OPPORTUNITIES 5
- How Bad Could the Outbreak Be? 8
- What Symptoms Should I Look Out For? 13
- How The Big Players Coped 15

CHAPTER 2 27
HEALTH - SYMPTOMS, HOSPITALISATIONS, RECOVERY STATISTICS, DEATH TOLL, VACCINATIONS 27
- COVID-19: A systemic crisis in human development 30
- When to seek Doctors help 39

CHAPTER 3 40
SOCIETY - LIVING UNDER COVID - WORK LIFE, QUALITY OF LIFE, TRAVEL BY AIR & SEA, WEARING MASKS EVEN AFTER VACCINATIONS ETC 40
- The propagation of the crisis to vulnerable groups 40
- The propagation of action to face COVID-19 43

CHAPTER 4 49
ECONOMY - COLLAPSE OF THE WORLD ECONOMY, RECOVERY, THE FUTURE, STOCK MARKET, WINNERS & LOSERS 49
- Economic shock: The 2008 global financial crisis 51
- Health shock: Ebola in West Africa 53
- Natural hazard shock: Hurricane Maria 54
- A human development perspective on how to respond to COVID-19 ... 55

CHAPTER 5 61
CONTROVERSY - LAB ACCIDENT FROM WUHAN, ON PURPOSE OR NOT, OTHER AGENCIES INVOLVEMENT MAYBE, CIA, CHINES SECURITY ETC. 61
- Safe space and balanced care work 65

- Inequality in public health and innovation systems............................68
- **CHAPTER 6**..**70**
  - DIFFERENT TYPES OF IMPACT OF COVID19 70
    - Disruption of the international postal supply chain............................88
- **CHAPTER 7**..**90**
  - IMPACT OF COVID-19 IN AFRICA 90
    - The View From Africa..95
    - Impact On Public Health 99
    - Economic Impact..101
    - Peace and security impacts 106
    - Adapting Democratic Participation To Covid-19............................108
- **CHAPTER 8**..**109**
  - COVID-19: MYSTERIES AND CONSPIRACIES.............................109
    - Trends of conspiracy theories vs. facts:..112
    - Political manipulation or how to use secret agenda: 116
- **CHAPTER 9**..**121**
  - THE GREAT ECONOMIC AND FINANCIAL RESET 121
    - IMPACT ON GLOBAL BUSINESS: 121
- **CHAPTER 10**..**133**
  - VACCINE DEVELOPED BY DIFFERENT PLAYERS 133
  - EFFORTS PUT IN PLACE BY COUNTRIES.................................138
- **CHAPTER 11**..**148**
  - WORKING FROM HOME AS THE NORMAL................................148
- **CONCLUSION** **153**

CHAPTER 1
HOW THE BIG PLAYERS COPED, CHINA, USA & INDIA. THE LOSERS & WINNERS, THE ROAD FORWARD FOR NEW OPPORTUNITIES

As 2019 drew to a close, reports emerged from an outbreak of unexplained etiology pneumonia, with cases clustered around Wuhan's Huanan Seafood Wholesale Market, China, that sold live fish, poultry, and birds. The patients were observed as of December 8th, and the cluster was first identified on December 31st. The market was being shut down on 1 January 2020, and on 7 January, a new type of coronavirus was officially detected by the Chinese authorities. All suspect cases found were checked by active case finding and retrospective examination. The belief was that over 300 people in Wuhan caught the infection of this new virus, and four died.

Also, the belief was that previous outbreaks of similar diseases, including SARS, have arisen from live animal markets. Camels transmit the coronavirus, which causes MERS to humans. The animal that was the source of the latest coronavirus is still unknown, and the collapse of Wuhan's meat market has made the matter almost impossible to investigate. Bats are a possible source because many viruses, including coronaviruses, have adapted to coexist. Nevertheless, it is very likely that the virus was transmitted to an intermediate species from the bats and then to humans.

Wuhan, an intense virology center in China, was well placed to diagnose and tackle the outbreak. However, it has brought China's disease preparedness to the test in a part of the world that still regularly remembers the 2003 extreme coronavirus outbreak of acute respiratory syndrome (SARS). The virus then spread from China to 25 other nations, infecting over 8,000 people and killing about 800 people before it got contained. In the present case, the Chinese authorities' pace announced the international community's outbreak was commendable and shows that lessons from previous attacks have been learned. As the international community reacts to an episode of coronavirus-induced pneumonia in Wuhan, China, early and transparent data sharing–essential to its protection–depends on the trust that the data will not be used without proper attribution.

What is Human Coronavirus, and How Dangerous Is It?

Coronaviruses are a large virus family usually targeting the respiratory organ. The name is derived from the Latin word corona, meaning crown, due to the spiky fringe surrounding these viruses. Many species, such as bats, cats, and birds, get sick. Just seven are known to infect humans like Covid-19, SARS, and MERS.

SARS is believed to have developed in China from bats to civet cats to humans; MERS has spread from bats to camels into Middle East humans. No one knows where the Covid-19 came from. For now, livestock in Wuhan, China, a town of 11 million, is thought to have taken the jump late last year. But scholars still seek to understand their exact roots. As for the signs, in 10 and more than 30 percent of cases, two of the seven coronaviruses that infect humans, SARS and MERS, can cause severe pneumonia and even death. The others, though, show milder effects, like a common cold. Covid-19 will kill — but it's not clear how often or how it relates the fatality rate to SARS and MERS.

According to the Centers for Disease Control and Prevention, most patients now start with fever, cough, and shortness of breath. An early analysis, published in The Lancet, offered even greater detail. It has looked at a subset of the first 41 patients in Wuhan with confirmed Covid-19. Fever, cough, muscle pain, and exhaustion were the most common symptoms; vomiting, nausea, and coughing up mucus or blood were less common. They all had CT scans of pneumonia and lung abnormalities. As for the severity of the disease: 13 people were taken to an ICU, where six died. By January 22, most patients had been discharged from the hospital (68 percent).

More recently, records have also been made of people with very mild symptoms, such as southern Germany. There is even evidence that events are asymptomatic. Covid-19 can likely look more like flu than it does like SARS. That's because when they are first detected, infectious diseases usually seem more severe. After all, people appearing in hospitals tend to be the sickest. However, the new virus seems less dangerous than both SARS and MERS.

How Bad Could the Outbreak Be?

The novel coronavirus, similar to SARS, seems highly contagious. The size of an epidemic depends on how quickly and easily viruses are transmitted. Although work has just started, scientists have estimated that every person with the new coronavirus could infect between 1.5 and 3.5 people elsewhere without successful containment measures. This would make the virus nearly as infectious as SARS, another coronavirus spread in China in 2003 and got contained after 8,098 people were sickened and 774 killed. Those respiratory viruses may move through the air, wrapped in tiny droplets formed when a sick person breathes, speaks, coughs, or sneezes. Some droplets fall within a few feet to the ground. This makes it harder for the virus to get, unlike viruses like measles, chickenpox, and tuberculosis, flying through the air for a hundred miles.

Nevertheless, detecting is better than H.I.V. or hepatitis, which only spreads by direct contact with an infected person's body fluids. Suppose each individual infected with the new coronavirus contaminates two to three other people. In that case, this may be sufficient to sustain and intensify an epidemic if there is no action taken to reduce it. Contrast that to a virus less infectious, like seasonal flu. Those with the flu appear, on average, to infect 1.3 other people.

The difference may seem slight, but the result is a striking contrast: Only about 45 people could be infected in the same situation. The number of cases outside of China has so far been limited. Yet reports have occurred in several countries in recent days, including the United States, of citizens who have not visited China. Besides, in 2003, the number of cases within China far exceeded the rate of SARS cases. The actual number of cases is almost definitely much greater than the number officially confirmed by laboratory tests.

Thousands of people were suspected of having been infected in Hubei province, where the epidemic started but was not diagnosed officially. Doctors say there's a shortage of test kits and other medical supplies, and residents say it's almost difficult to get the health care they need to treat the coronavirus — or even diagnose it—. Various epidemiological models predict the total number of cases to be 100,000 or more. Experts have urged caution when calculating these figures.

How Deadly Is The Virus?

It is still hard to know. Perhaps the fatality rate is less than 3 percent, however, much fewer than SARS. This is one of the utmost significant factors, and one of the least known, in how destructive the outbreak will be. Assessing the lethality of a new virus is challenging. The worst cases are usually first identified, which may distort our perception of how patients are likely to die. Around one-third of Wuhan's first 41 patients had to be treated in an ICU, many with fever symptoms, severe cough, shortness of breath, and pneumonia. But people with mild cases are never allowed to visit a doctor.

There may be more deaths than we know; therefore, the death rate may be lower than we initially thought.

At the same time, there may be underreported deaths from the virus. The Chinese cities at the heart of the outbreak face a shortage of test kits and hospital beds, and many sick people could not see a doctor. There is still a lot of uncertainty about the existence of this virus and what it is doing. Early indications show that this virus's fatality rate is significantly lower than that of another coronavirus, MERS, which kills about 35 percent of infected people, and SARS, which kills about 10 percent. All the diseases tend to bind on proteins on the lung cell surface, but MERS and SARS seem to be more harmful to lung tissue.

Of China's 17,000 people infected, 82% had moderate infections, 15% had severe symptoms, and 3% were listed as critical. A lower than 2 percent had died from confirmed cases. Many of those that died were older men with underlying health issues. The virus causes severe respiratory disease (i.e., pneumonia) and death from mild symptoms. Many deaths occurred in people over the age of 65 and were also suffering from another chronic condition or illness. Data suggest a case-fatality rate of about 2 percent (meaning two deaths out of every 100 confirmed cases), even though it is still too early to give a reliable cipher. If the number of undiagnosed asymptomatic cases or cases with very mild symptoms becomes high, it could be lower. If the virus mutates, it could intensify. In any case, the fatality rate is lower compared to SARS (10%) and higher than that of seasonal flu (less than 0.01%).

Where Has the Virus Spread?

We still don't know how exactly Covid-19 spreads, but we do have a lot of data on how MERS, SARS, and other respiratory viruses travel from person to individual. This is primarily by exposure to droplets caused by sneezing or coughing. When sick individual coughs or sneezes, they let out a mist, and when those droplets touch another person's nose, eyes, or mouth, they will pass on the virus. In rare cases, a person can indirectly catch a respiratory illness "by touching droplets on surfaces— and then touching mucosal membranes" in the mouth, eyes, and nose. This is why handwashing is an important measure of public health and particularly in an outbreak.

The virus rapidly spreads because it began in a transport hub. Wuhan is a hard place to get an outbreak; it has 11 million people, more than the City of New York. On a typical day, 3,500 passengers take direct flights to towns in other countries from Wuhan. Those cities were among the first outside of China to record virus cases. Wuhan is also a major transportation center within China, linked by high-speed trains and domestic airlines to Beijing, Shanghai, and other major cities. Up to two million people flew from Wuhan to different places inside China in October and November last year.

During the SARS outbreak in 2003, China had not been nearly as well associated. Large numbers of migrant workers are now moving domestically and internationally— to Africa, other parts of Asia, and Latin America. China's Belt and Road Initiative is making a considerable infrastructure drive. This travel poses a high risk of outbreaks in countries with health-care systems not equipped to handle them, such as Zimbabwe, which is facing a growing hunger and economic crisis.

Furthermore, China has about four times as many passengers on the train and air as it did during the SARS outbreak. China took the unprecedented step of enforcing travel restrictions on tens of millions of people living in Wuhan and surrounding towns. However, experts cautioned that the lockout might have come too late, with restricted access to food and medication. Wuhan's mayor confirmed that five million people had left the city in the Lunar New Year's run-up before the restrictions began.

The Mode of Transmission

The Transmission Mode Much of how Covid-19, a new coronavirus, spreads is unclear. Current awareness came mainly from what the world knows of related coronaviruses. Coronaviruses are a large family of viruses commonly found in many different animal species, including camels, goats, cats, and bats. Rarely can animal coronaviruses infect people and spread among people, including MERS, SARS, and now with Covid-19. Most respiratory viruses get transmitted by sneezing and coughing. Although the Chinese authorities initially played down the possibility of human-to-human transmission, substantial and sustained communication among people has now become apparent. Chinese scientists have cautioned that some infected people may transmit the virus to others even before developing illness or experiencing any symptoms. However, a published study documenting asymptomatic transmission in Germany has been criticized as inaccurate.

If the virus can be spread by individuals with no symptoms at all or mild symptoms due to respiratory disease— including headache or backache—that is terrible. They're up and about, going to work or the gym or religious services, and breathing on or touching other people when people don't know they're sick. The spreading from person to person happens within close contacts (about 6 feet). The initial thought was that spreading from person to person occurs primarily through respiratory droplets created when an infected person coughs or sneezes, similar to how influenza and other respiratory pathogens spread. Such droplets may land in nearby people's mouths or noses or probably be inhaled into the lungs. Whether a person can get Covid19 by touching a surface or object with the virus on it and then touching their mouth, nose, or probably eyes, is currently unclear. Usually, people are thought to be most infected with most respiratory viruses when they're most symptomatic (the sickest).

It is important to note that the ease with which a virus spreads will vary from person to person. Many viruses (such as measles) are highly contagious, while other viruses are less so. There's much more to learn about the transmissibility, frequency, and other characteristics of Covid19 and ongoing investigations. This information will help the risk assessment further.

What Symptoms Should I Look Out For?

Symptoms of this infection include fever, heavy cough, and breathing difficulties or shortness of breath. The disease triggers pneumonia and lung lesions. Mild cases may mimic flu or a bad cold, making it challenging to identify. Patients might be familiar with other symptoms, such as gastrointestinal issues or diarrhea. It is known that the incubation period— the duration from exposure to the onset of symptoms — is anywhere from 10 days to two weeks.

See your health care provider if you have a fever or cough and have recently visited China or spent time with someone who did. Call first, so they can plan for your visit and take steps to prevent potential exposure to other patients and staff.

How Time-consuming Does It Take To Reveal Symptoms?

The new coronavirus novel shows symptoms ranging from 2 to 14 days, enabling the disease to go undetected. Reported conditions have run from people with little to no signs to severely sick people and dying with reported Covid-19 infections. Symptoms may include:

- Fever
- Cough
- Shortness of breath

This is dependent on what was historically known as the MERS virus incubation period. The amount of time it takes for signs to occur after an infected person can be critical for prevention and control.

Identified as the duration of incubation, this time helps health officials to isolate or track individuals who may have been exposed to the virus. Nevertheless, if the incubation period is too long or too short, it may be challenging to implement such steps.

A lot of disease, such as influenza, have a brief two to the three-day incubation period. People can shed infectious virus particles until they show flu symptoms, making it highly difficult to recognize and isolate people who have the virus. Nevertheless, SARS had an incubation period of about five days. It also took four to five days after symptoms started before it becomes transmittable to sick people, which gave officials time to stop the infection and contain the outbreak effectively.

Executives at the Centers for Disease Regulator and Prevention say the incubation period for the current coronavirus is 2-14 days. But whether a person can spread the virus before symptoms occur is still not clear, or whether the nature of the disease influences how quickly a patient can spread the virus. This is troubling because it may mean the identification of the infection will elude.

How The Big Players Coped
CHINA

At the time, the wider world was shocked by the harsh restrictions and rigid enforcement. From late January until June, the city was effectively sealed off from the rest of the country.

But even though it came at a significant cost, it proved to be a highly successful method of tackling the virus.

One year on, China is often held up as one of the virus success stories - not least by Beijing itself. So how exactly did China get from lockdown to here - and how has Beijing controlled its own story?

Authorities were slow to react to initial reports of a mystery illness circulating at a wet market in Wuhan in late 2019, allowing millions of the city's residents to move around the country in the days leading up to Chinese New Year, a traditional high-travel period, in January 2020.

Earlier this week, an interim report by an independent panel appointed by the World Health Organization (WHO) criticized China's initial response, saying that "public health measures could have been applied more forcefully".

But once China finally recognized there was a problem, authorities cracked down hard.

On January 23, two days before the country celebrated Chinese New Year, the streets of Wuhan fell silent: some 11 million people were put under tight quarantine, and face masks and social distancing became mandatory.

With medical capacities overwhelmed, authorities surprised the world as they managed to set up entire field hospitals within days.

But even so, residents like Wenjun Wang were scared. She told the BBC at the time how her uncle had already died, and her parents were sick - but getting help was still all but impossible.

The methods used in Wuhan would become routinely employed in the following months as China tackled outbreaks in other major cities such as Beijing and Shanghai with immediate lockdowns and swift mass testing.

Entry into China, meanwhile, was managed by tight entry and quarantine control. But even in those early days, authorities also sought to tightly control the spread of information - an issue which would crop up again and again over the next year, and an issue our colleagues examined in December.

Doctors who tried to warn each other about the virus were reprimanded and ordered to keep silent. The most famous of these, Dr Li Wenliang, died himself later from the virus. News outlets, which initially were allowed some room to report from Wuhan, faced a clampdown while citizen journalists who tried to report from the city were silenced. Recently, one of them received a four-year prison sentence.

While China's rigorous lockdowns may have initially struck observers as harsh and restrictive, the official data one year on appears to justify the measures, with a comparatively low death toll and caseload.

China has had just under 100,000 recorded infections, with only around 4,800 deaths linked to Covid-19. Unlike many other countries, after the initial outbreak, the numbers appear to flatline with no second wave in sight.

Chinese data however does not include asymptomatic cases in this particular tally and some observers have raised doubts over its reliability.

However, censorship has made it difficult to get a full sense of how Wuhan, and other parts of the country, coped with the strict measures.

What is certain is that this past year has taken a psychological toll, according to recent interviews with Wuhan residents, some of whom were worried about talking to international media.

"The pandemic has certainly left something behind, even if it is not visible on the surface," one resident, Han Meimei, told the BBC.

"But there is certainly trauma deep inside many people in this city, including many details of the past year that I don't think I wanted to look at clearly until now." Still, there is a feeling among some Chinese - helped by state propaganda - that China has handled the pandemic better than most, as some Beijing residents told the BBC recently.

And for others, there is now a greater sense of unity and connection.

A Wuhan student, who only wanted to be known as Li Xi, said: "Before the pandemic, everyone seemed a bit grumpy, often rushed... but after the pandemic, they have become more grateful for life and much more warm-hearted."

"This kind of disaster has actually brought more people together," said Han. "If people are there, the city is still there."

Authorities remain on alert for any new outbreaks - recent ones in Qingdao and Kashgar resulted in swift quarantines and mass testing.

While case numbers have remained very low, in recent weeks an uptick in cases has worried authorities. Earlier this month, China saw its largest increase in daily case numbers in five months.

Officials are now focused on the north east, with an estimated 19 million people currently under lockdown in the region including the city of Shijiazhuang as well as parts of Hebei, Jilin and Heilongjiang provinces.

The pandemic and the periodic lockdowns have had a significant impact on the economy, Millions of jobs have been lost and China saw its slowest growth in more than four decades, although it began recovering quickly and was the only major world economy to grow in 2020.

But in theory, life is almost back to normal in vast swathes of China, and - a year on - the focus is once again on Chinese New Year, and the fact millions of people are preparing to travel home.

There are, of course, fears that chunyun, the mass travel period around Chinese New Year, will become a super spreader event when it officially begins late next week. As a result, all eyes are currently on the vaccination programme.

Chinese companies Sinovac and Sinopharm received domestic emergency approvals for their vaccines in mid-2020 and began administering them to employees, frontline workers and paying members of the public even before clinical trials were completed. In October a BBC team filmed hundreds rushing to get vaccinated.

Reports of their efficiency vary widely. Chinese officials have said they are aiming to inoculate 50 million people before chunyun.

Beijing is also seeking to steer the narrative about the origin and cause of the global pandemic.

There have been accusations that authorities sought to cover up the severity of outbreak during its early days.

China, however, started saying that although Wuhan was where the first cluster was detected, it may not necessarily be the location where the virus originated from.

State media has recently suggested the pandemic might have begun outside of China - Spain, Italy or even the US - and have also carried claims that the virus has been entering the country through frozen food imports, though experts have cast doubt on this.

Last year, the BBC went to Wuhan to trace how the first cluster emerged and talk to those who lost loved ones in the initial outbreak.

This month, a team sent by the World Health Organization finally arrived in Wuhan to find out how the virus originated, amid concerns over what kind of data and access will be given by the Chinese authorities.

Observers are also worried that with international investigations taking place only one year after the initial outbreak in Wuhan, answers may still prove to be elusive.

USA

Everyone anticipated that the United States of America would be rapid and effective in terms of response to Covid-19. However, this has not happened for the United States. It is now host to more documented COVID-19 cases and deaths than any other country.

With about 4% of the world's population, the US accounts for about 25% of all cases and about 20% of all deaths — more than 169,000 deaths so far.

Yes, it's a large country, but that is about 500 deaths per million population, compared with Australia's about 12 per million.

The firsthand experience since the beginning of Covid-19, the US have shown how deficiencies in the organisation of the US social, political and health-care systems have become more vivid and their consequences intensified.

Given its status as a world superpower, and its stratospheric per capita health care spend, the situation in the US is truly alarming.

Entire books will be written on this woeful epoch in US history. But I want to focus on some key observations of the country's failed COVID-19 response, and the lessons.

Given how Donald Trump's administration handled the situation, it would be largely unfair to label him as the sole cause of how Covid-19 ravaged the US. President Donald Trump and his administration may be the poster boy for the systemic failures in the US social and health-care systems. The basic truth is that those issues have been decades in the making.

But his pre-COVID-19 dismantling of the pandemic preparedness system, disregard for scientists, and hyper-partisanship have clearly worsened the US response. David Frum said that "That the pandemic occurred is not Trump's fault. The utter unpreparedness of the United States for a pandemic is Trump's fault."

President Barack Obama left the Trump administration with pandemic-ready infrastructure. This was motivated by outbreaks of Ebola and previous novel coronaviruses (responsible for Middle East Respiratory Syndrome, or MERS, and SARS, severe acute respiratory syndrome), and an appreciation of their ever-present threat.

Then, Trump took critical steps before COVID-19 that weakened its preparedness to the point of catastrophe. Here are just a few.

The Trump administration dismantled the (Obama-instituted) White House team in charge of pandemic response, dismissing its leadership and staff in early 2018. This team had also laid out a detailed dossier for a pandemic response plan. Trump ignored it.

Since coming to office, the Trump administration has also cut funding to key agencies including the Centers for Disease Control and Prevention (CDC). These cuts directly impacted domestic projects and international collaborations (including with China) on pandemic preparedness.

Even into February as the severity of the pandemic was realised worldwide, Trump was downplaying the threat, openly stating it was like the common flu.

He called growing concerns about COVID-19 a "hoax" and had a "hunch" expert assessments of the potential toll were wrong.

As cases and deaths, particularly in New York began to rise steeply, the real evidence of unpreparedness became apparent.

Critically, at no point through the pandemic has the US had in place a sincere strategy of public health 101: test, trace, isolate.

Trump has repeatedly claimed anyone who wants a test can get a test, but this has been a farce. Shortages of testing supplies and poor coordination have hamstrung containment strategies.

Even though testing has increased, it has not kept up with demand. The time to receive results as of July ranged from 1 to 14 days, averaging 7 days.

This is inadequate to manage spread via active but undiagnosed cases. That is just the beginning of the current troubles.

The limited availability of masks, personal protective equipment (PPE) and ventilators revealed significant cracks in US preparedness. It also put on full display the caustic political divisions that are a modern feature of US politics and society.

Despite the first cases being recorded in Washington state, its deadly potential was initially felt most in the Democratic state of New York. Trump used this to avenge old scores and fuel competition between red (Republican) versus blue (Democratic) states.

When the New York health-care system buckled as a result of its fragmented structure (another failing) and enormous caseload, the state's Democratic governor, Andrew Cuomo, called for urgent assistance, such as supplies from the national stockpile.

Trump tweeted Governor Cuomo "should spend more time 'doing' and less time 'complaining'."

The fierce competition between states for limited mask and PPE supplies led to suppliers price-gouging.

Frustration led governors to place clandestine international orders. Illinois and Maryland, for example, received plane-loads of supplies under the cloak of darkness and protected by state police. They did this "out of fear the Trump administration would seize the cargo for the federal stockpile", as occurred in Massachusetts.

There has also been tension across the country about stay-at-home orders, school closures, schools and retail reopenings, data transparency and sharing – the list goes on.

Wearing a mask has become a political act. Now, concerningly, Trump has ordered COVID-related hospital data bypass the CDC and be fed directly to the White House, raising concerns about transparency.

Despite Trump threatening his absolute authority over the states, much responsibility rests with state governors (equivalent to Australian premiers). And yet counties (equivalent to local councils) have enacted policies independent of, and often contradicting, state policies.

This could be sensible in reflecting local conditions as the rolling wave moves on. However, it has confused any singular messaging and exemplified the red/blue political divide.

The southern (primarily red) states that were late to institute control measures and early to re-open are now the epicentre of this rolling wave.

Systematic Inequality

Among OECD countries, the level of structural inequality in the US is extreme. The collision of three problems — uncontrolled pandemic, recession, uninsured people — is disproportionately impacting the most vulnerable.

Pre-pandemic, about 32 million Americans (around 10% of population) lacked health insurance. A further 150 million (around 50% of the population) held employer-sponsored health insurance.

Up to July 18, about 32 million Americans had filed for unemployment as a direct result of the pandemic, pushing the unemployment rate well into teen figures.

This number is rising weekly and millions of those have, or will, lose their employer-sponsored health insurance at a time they may need it most.

The US has the unenviable first place position for the highest health-care costs in the OECD yet some the worst health outcomes among similar countries.

COVID-19 has placed millions more Americans further away from accessing needed health care.

The country was already experiencing a decline in life expectancy and the fear now is this will be exacerbated further.

India

A deadly wave of COVID-19 is overwhelming India: New cases have hit 400,000+ per day, and more than 215,000 people have lost their lives.

The health system is buckling under demand, but we're helping families reach vaccinations as we work in close contact with health workers who need masks, COVID-19 test kits, and disinfectant to save lives and stay safe. Our work in India — and the 20+ countries we serve — will not be over until these nations have resilient health systems that can serve their populations, in times of crisis and every day after. Your recurring gift, started now, will go straight toward this work, first in India, then across the world.

CHAPTER 2
HEALTH - SYMPTOMS, HOSPITALISATIONS, RECOVERY STATISTICS, DEATH TOLL, VACCINATIONS

The United Nations has called the COVID-19 pandemic "the greatest test that we have faced since the formation of the United Nations," 7 clarifying that it is more than a health emergency. It is a systemic crisis already affecting economies and societies in unprecedented ways. The managing director of the International Monetary Fund has anticipated "the worst economic fallout since the Great Depression. Just [in January 2020], we expected positive per capita income growth in over 160 of our member countries in 2020. Today, [in mid-April 2020] that number has been turned on its head: we now project that over 170 countries will experience negative per capita income growth this year."

It is becoming an acute social crisis in many parts of the world, affecting people's lives in multiple ways, including a surge in violence against women and disruption in jobs and livelihoods. Most countries have made tremendous progress dealing with relatively frequent shocks, thanks to continuous learning and preparedness through policies and social norms. However, the ability to respond to very rare or even new shocks is much lower and unequally distributed. Indeed, the 2019 Human Development Report highlighted that among the new generation of capabilities for the 21st century was the resilience to low frequency but very high impact shocks.

Countries worldwide have put in motion a broad set of measures to handle COVID-19 on several fronts. Learning occurs through research, the study of other communities' experiences, and a fair dose of trial and error. Policies changing people's behavior have been central in response to contain the virus's spread: Billions of people have got the call to stay at home. Beyond the ongoing response, action over the next few weeks and months will have lasting effects on people's lives and the perceptions of national and multilateral institutions' ability to drive human development.

This note explores four arguments. First, this is a systemic human development crisis—affecting health, economic, and broad social dimensions of development and potentially eroding gains accumulated over decades. The note shows the compounding effects on health, education, and the economy and how responses have to be considered in a context where economic and social activities are being restricted for public health reasons.

Second, without appropriate policies in place, the indirect effects of the crisis can be taxing or even more taxing than the direct health effects. History shows that problems—even short-lived ones—have a long-term impact on people's human development that are often difficult to monitor and anticipate, but the distribution is unequal. COVID-19 is unlikely to be an exception.

Third, investments in advancing and reducing social development disparities are crucial to ensure a timely recovery and prepare for the next crisis. From a human development perspective, concerned with expanding people's capabilities, protecting public health, and sustaining living standards are essential. Advancing and reducing disparities in both primary and enhanced capabilities—the new necessities of the 21st century, as defined in the 2019 Human Development Report—are crucial to achieving both goals.

Fourth, this systemic crisis attacks a world dealing with unresolved tensions: between people and technology, people and planet, and between the haves and the have-nots—all of which are shaping a new generation of inequalities. But the response to the crisis is an opportunity to reimagine how those tensions get tackled.

COVID-19: A systemic crisis in human development

This is not the first time that humanity is facing a pandemic. The Black Death upended the structures of economies and societies in medieval Europe. To protect travel and commerce, Italy pioneered quarantines and other containment measures during the Renaissance. In the early 19th century, global outbreaks of cholera led to unprecedented global cooperation on public health in international sanitary conferences during the middle of the 19th century.

Almost exactly 100 years ago, broad movements of people worldwide in the aftermath of World War I contributed to the spread of an influenza virus that led to one of the most lethal pandemics on record: the 1918 Flu pandemic. And a little over ten years ago, hundreds of thousands of people died during the H1N1 pandemic. Recent outbreaks of new zoonotic (meaning, that jump from non-human animals to humans) diseases (SARS, MERS) had significant impacts in many parts of the world, as did outbreaks of already known zoonotic diseases (Ebola). AIDS has caused more than 32 million deaths since the early 1980s.

But this pandemic has been unprecedented because it evolved from a health shock to an economic and social crisis. Social distancing and the pause in nonessential business have slowed human activities. The International Labour Organization projects that in the second quarter of 2020, working hours will fall by the equivalent of 195 million full-time workers. Unlike other crises, employment is being hit through two main channels. A contraction in labor demand comes from reduced human activity and the wealth effects of the global recession. A short-term drop in labor supply comes from the suspension of nonessential productive activities in several countries. The curtailment of labor Enhanced capabilities to supply and increase in unemployment call for appropriate macroeconomic policy. But the effects go beyond the typical decline in aggregate demand that is usually addressed by stimulating consumption and encouraging economic activity.

This is because the public health policies to slow the spread of COVID-19 are premised on reducing human interaction and—as a result—economic activity. These effects are intertwined with varying propagation patterns. The financial shock can hit countries before the health shock, through income effects, and persist after the health crisis. Or even when labor supply restrictions are lifted, hours worked can remain reduced because of slow recovery in mobility or depressed consumer demand. This calls for novel approaches.

In practice, very high human development countries (for the most part) suffered the health shock first, with the response based on robust health systems and supportive monetary and fiscal policies. Developing economies (with some exceptions, such as China and Singapore) are being affected by COVID-19 with a lag. The health crisis is still evolving, and the projection is that developing countries will get heavily affected during the rest of 2020. As an aggravating factor, they are entering the process in the middle of a global economic collapse and rising uncertainty (including in health security, food security, and job security), and they have weaker structural conditions with which to cope.

These shock hit a world wealthier than at any other time yet confronting profound divide in human turn growth—influencing weakness to and readiness for emergencies. It is too soon for a far reaching evaluation of the results of COVID-19 on human development. Yet, it is conceivable to assess the feasible consequences for individuals' capacities utilizing a rendition of the Human Development Index (HDI) that is more delicate to the effect of COVID-19. This changed index holds the standard HDI measurements however alters the training markers to mirror the impacts of school closures and moderation measures. What makes a difference for abilities is whether understudies are occupied with instructive exercises, which rely upon physical and virtual (web based) admittance to schools and learning assets. The changed index additionally utilizes the International Monetary Fund (IMF) projections of gross public pay per capita for 2020. Life expectancy at birth in 2020 (based on the United Nations Department of Economic and Social Affairs' 2019 Revision of World Population Prospects) is adjusted by the potential effects of COVID-19 on human health. By using the low-impact scenario from a recent study published in The Lancet Global Health for child mortality. Under this scenario, the global life expectancy at birth in 2020 expects to be around its level in 2019.

While not all schools are closed worldwide, many are, and simulations using the COVID-19-adjusted HDI projects a steep decline in human development worldwide in 2020. A massive setback led to this ineffective education because of school closures affecting almost 9 in 10 students and deep recessions in most economies (including a 4 percent drop in GNI per capita worldwide). The decline in the index – reflecting the narrowing of capabilities-- would be equivalent to erasing all the progress in human development of the past six years. The simulations' results point to a shock in powers that would be unprecedented since the concept of social development was introduced in 1990. If conditions in school access are restored, capabilities related to education would immediately bounce back – while the income dimension would follow the path of the economic recovery post-crisis.

The simulations assume a fast recovery during the second half of 2020, following IMF projections, and count on the full normalization of schools. They do not take into account potential indirect effects. Access to new technologies influences the impact of the crisis and the quality of the recovery. Two scenarios show the importance of enhanced capabilities.

First, without any internet access, the decline in human development would be 2.5 times worse. The comparison with this scenario of how technology is already providing mitigation mechanisms. Second, with more equitable access to the internet—where countries close the gap with leaders in their development group, something doable—the decline is more than halved. The key to facing these shocks is to empower people to accommodate the measures needed to deal with the crisis (including the physical closure of schools and workplaces).

Symptoms

Coronaviruses are a family of viruses that can cause illnesses such as the common cold, severe acute respiratory syndrome (SARS) and Middle East respiratory syndrome (MERS). In 2019, a new coronavirus was identified as the cause of a disease outbreak that originated in China.

The virus is now known as the severe acute respiratory syndrome coronavirus 2 (SARS-CoV-2). The disease it causes is called coronavirus disease 2019 (COVID-19). In March 2020, the World Health Organization (WHO) declared the COVID-19 outbreak a pandemic.

Public health groups, including the U.S. Centers for Disease Control and Prevention (CDC) and WHO, are monitoring the pandemic and posting updates on their websites. These groups have also issued recommendations for preventing and treating the illness.

Signs and symptoms of coronavirus disease 2019 (COVID-19) may appear two to 14 days after exposure. This time after exposure and before having symptoms is called the incubation period. Common signs and symptoms can include:

- Fever
- Cough
- Tiredness

- Early symptoms of COVID-19 may include a loss of taste or smell.

Other symptoms can include:

- Shortness of breath or difficulty breathing
- Muscle aches
- Chills
- Sore throat
- Runny nose
- Headache
- Chest pain
- Pink eye (conjunctivitis)
- Nausea
- Vomiting
- Diarrhea
- Rash

This list is not all inclusive. Children have similar symptoms to adults and generally have mild illness.

The severity of COVID-19 symptoms can range from very mild to severe. Some people may have only a few symptoms, and some people may have no symptoms at all. Some people may experience worsened symptoms, such as worsened shortness of breath and pneumonia, about a week after symptoms start.

People who are older have a higher risk of serious illness from COVID-19, and the risk increases with age. People who have existing medical conditions also may have a higher risk of serious illness. Certain medical conditions that may increase the risk of serious illness from COVID-19 include:

Serious heart diseases, such as heart failure, coronary artery disease or cardiomyopathy

- Cancer
- Chronic obstructive pulmonary disease (COPD)
- Type 1 or type 2 diabetes
- Overweight, obesity or severe obesity
- High blood pressure
- Smoking
- Chronic kidney disease
- Sickle cell disease or thalassemia
- Weakened immune system from solid organ transplants
- Pregnancy
- Asthma
- Chronic lung diseases such as cystic fibrosis or pulmonary fibrosis
- Liver disease
- Dementia
- Down syndrome

- Weakened immune system from bone marrow transplant, HIV or some medications
- Brain and nervous system conditions
- Substance use disorders

This list is not all inclusive. Other underlying medical conditions may increase your risk of serious illness from COVID-19.

If you have COVID-19 signs or symptoms or you've been in contact with someone diagnosed with COVID-19, contact your doctor or clinic right away for medical advice. Tell your health care team about your symptoms and possible exposure before you go to your appointment.

If you have emergency COVID-19 signs and symptoms, seek care immediately. Emergency signs and symptoms can include:

- Trouble breathing
- Persistent chest pain or pressure
- Inability to stay awake
- New confusion
- Pale, gray or blue-colored skin, lips or nail beds — depending on skin tone

This list isn't all inclusive. Let your doctor know if you are an older adult or have chronic medical conditions, such as heart disease or lung disease, as you may have a greater risk of becoming seriously ill with COVID-19. During the pandemic, it's important to make sure health care is available for those in greatest need.

If you have COVID-19 signs or symptoms or you've been in contact with someone diagnosed with COVID-19, contact your doctor or clinic right away for medical advice. Tell your health care team about your symptoms and possible exposure before you go to your appointment.

If you have emergency COVID-19 signs and symptoms, seek care immediately. Emergency signs and symptoms can include:

- Trouble breathing
- Persistent chest pain or pressure
- Inability to stay awake
- New confusion
- Pale, gray or blue-colored skin, lips or nail beds — depending on skin tone

Risk factors for COVID-19 appear to include:

Close contact (within 6 feet, or 2 meters) with someone who has COVID-19

Being coughed or sneezed on by an infected person

When to seek Doctors help

If you have COVID-19 signs or symptoms or you've been in contact with someone diagnosed with COVID-19, contact your doctor or clinic right away for medical advice. Tell your health care team about your symptoms and possible exposure before you go to your appointment.

If you have emergency COVID-19 signs and symptoms, seek care immediately. Emergency signs and symptoms can include:

- Trouble breathing
- Persistent chest pain or pressure
- Inability to stay awake
- New confusion
- Pale, gray or blue-colored skin, lips or nail beds — depending on skin tone

This list isn't all inclusive. Let your doctor know if you are an older adult or have chronic medical conditions, such as heart disease or lung disease, as you may have a greater risk of becoming seriously ill with COVID-19. During the pandemic, it's important to make sure health care is available for those in greatest need.

CHAPTER 3
SOCIETY - LIVING UNDER COVID - WORK LIFE, QUALITY OF LIFE, TRAVEL BY AIR & SEA, WEARING MASKS EVEN AFTER VACCINATIONS ETC

The propagation of the crisis to vulnerable groups

Some negative impacts of COVID-19 are being felt harder by individual countries and by groups within countries. For instance, once the health crisis escalated in a few countries in Asia and Europe, developing countries started to experience the effects of economic contagion before any noticeable impact on public health from the virus itself. Some of the impacts in the developing world hit even before COVID-19 contagion, through different channels:

• Financial channels. Short-term capital outflows have been massive—even more significant than in the 2008 global financial crisis. Capital flight has been particularly intense in China (also driven by a sharp drop in international oil prices). According to the United Nations

Conference on Trade and Development, sovereign credit spreads for emerging markets (reflecting country risk assessments) have been following the 2008 financial crisis's rising pattern.

• Trade channels. Commodity prices (significant for developing countries) have plummeted. Both oil and nonoil prices have fallen more than during the 2008 financial crisis—though factors other than COVID-19 were important in the drop in oil prices. The cumulative decline in both is over 50 percent. International services (travel and tourism) have also been severely affected.

• Migration and remittances. Many countries have restricted movement across borders. Migrant workers—who often face precarious conditions in host countries—are likely to experience job losses and income declines, affecting remittances to their families in developing countries.

This pandemic is a challenge for every country. But in countries with high inequalities by class, age, gender, ethnicity, or residence status, the effects can amplify these differences, at least in the short run. Within countries, certain groups are already being disproportionately affected: older people, women, young workers, migrant households, unprotected workers, people living in shelters, people who are homeless or in informal settlements, and people with underlying health issues. Comorbidities appear to exacerbate the virus's negative impact, with underlying health issues related to social vulnerability: Health issues tend to be more prevalent among people from ethnic minorities or low-income groups.

In most vulnerable households, income often depends on one person, increasing the household's risk of falling into poverty. The number of people expected to live in extreme poverty is projected to increase by 40-60 million using the IMF's economic growth for 2020 as the primary benchmark. The number of undernourished people could increase by 14–80 million.

The pandemic is exposing the disadvantages already faced by low-income groups—and magnifying fissures. For instance, social distancing directives to not physically be at the workplace have dramatically unequal implications. People with higher incomes are more likely to work from home—and thus to continue to have earnings and stay healthy. People in low-income groups are more likely to be in "essential" occupations —that require workers to come to the workplace and risk exposure to infection. A study based on mobile devices in the United States shows that people in wealthier groups stay home more than people in low-income groups. In metro areas with the most significant disparities between rich and poor, people in high-income neighborhoods stopped moving right after official guidance. People in lower-income neighborhoods reduced movement as well, but later and only partially.

The propagation of action to face COVID-19
Nonpharmaceutical interventions

In the absence of a vaccine or therapeutics, most of the measures to slow the spread of COVID-19 have been nonpharmaceutical interventions. The strategy of reducing contagion aims to protect the most vulnerable populations and avoid excessive pressure on health systems. Even countries with high numbers of hospital beds per 1,000 people can see health services become overwhelmed during the peak of a pandemic. So, reducing virus transmission reduces the health system's pressure and health workers, buying them time to increase and spread capacity.

Measures related to movement and travel affect tourism and other services as well as global supply chains. By mid-April, more than 1.4 billion children ages 5–17 in 147 countries (or 86 percent of children worldwide) were out of school.

Economic measures

While it is too soon to assess the pandemic's economic impact, it is already being described as the worst plunge in economic activity since the Great Depression. In response, as of early-May 2020, most countries had implemented emergency monetary and fiscal measures, and numerous countries had also implemented trade and balance of payments measures. More than $8 trillion has been committed to fighting the crisis across the world on the fiscal front. In addition to new resources directed to boost health system responses, economic policies have been tailored to support the household, business, and financial sectors40 by addressing both solvency (by providing various subsidies and cash transfers, supporting unemployment insurance mechanisms and offering equity guarantees) and liquidity (by giving credit through multiple channels, postponing tax or financial obligations and purchasing assets).

On the monetary front, central banks have cut interest rates.42 Given the limited space for conventional monetary policy in an environment of low-interest rates, major central banks have resorted to quantitative easing (buying credit instruments in open markets) and other interventions to keep credit markets liquid. There has also been significant international cooperation among monetary authorities. In March 2020, the central banks of Canada, England, Japan, Switzerland, and Europe announced swap facilities, increasing the frequency of maturity operations to boost liquidity.

And the US Federal Reserve extended liquidity arrangements with Australia, Brazil, the Republic of Korea, Mexico, Singapore, and Sweden to provide US dollar liquidity. The response on the economic front is still unfolding, with developed countries leading. By mid-April 2020, 96 percent of very high human development countries had announced a policy package, compared with 85 percent of high human development countries, 78 percent of medium human development countries, and 73 percent of low social development countries. The scale of a country's policies depends on its level of human development. The average fiscal package based on direct programs accounts for 4.9 percent of GDP in very high human development countries but 1 percent of GDP in low and medium human development countries. The pattern is similar for loans and guarantees.

The immense financial cost of these measures during a time of recession and depressed fiscal revenues will result in higher fiscal deficits and public debts. This will bring short-term financial restrictions to deal with liquidity needs and long-term economic vulnerability linked to solvency mitigation, given the context of low-interest rates. Still, credit spreads are opening up, so there is a risk of debt crises without appropriate measures, as the United Nations Secretary-General called for. In early April 2020, 90 countries had called for emergency financing from the IMF. Financial mechanisms—globally coordinated—are needed. Their effectiveness will depend mainly on their ability to strengthen people's capabilities in the long term.

Symptoms

Signs and symptoms of coronavirus disease 2019 (COVID-19) may appear two to 14 days after exposure. This time after exposure and before having symptoms is called the incubation period. Common signs and symptoms can include:

- Fever
- Cough
- Tiredness

- Early symptoms of COVID-19 may include a loss of taste or smell.

Other symptoms can include:

- Shortness of breath or difficulty breathing
- Muscle aches
- Chills
- Sore throat
- Runny nose
- Headache
- Chest pain
- Pink eye (conjunctivitis)
- Nausea
- Vomiting
- Diarrhea
- Rash

This list is not all inclusive. Children have similar symptoms to adults and generally have mild illness.

The severity of COVID-19 symptoms can range from very mild to severe. Some people may have only a few symptoms, and some people may have no symptoms at all. Some people may experience worsened symptoms, such as worsened shortness of breath and pneumonia, about a week after symptoms start.

People who are older have a higher risk of serious illness from COVID-19, and the risk increases with age. People who have existing medical conditions also may have a higher risk of serious illness. Certain medical conditions that may increase the risk of serious illness from COVID-19 include:

Serious heart diseases, such as heart failure, coronary artery disease or cardiomyopathy

- Cancer
- Chronic obstructive pulmonary disease (COPD)
- Type 1 or type 2 diabetes
- Overweight, obesity or severe obesity
- High blood pressure
- Smoking
- Chronic kidney disease
- Sickle cell disease or thalassemia
- Weakened immune system from solid organ transplants
- Pregnancy
- Asthma
- Chronic lung diseases such as cystic fibrosis or pulmonary fibrosis
- Liver disease
- Dementia
- Down syndrome

- Weakened immune system from bone marrow transplant, HIV or some medications
- Brain and nervous system conditions
- Substance use disorders

This list is not all inclusive. Other underlying medical conditions may increase your risk of serious illness from COVID-19.

CHAPTER 4
ECONOMY - COLLAPSE OF THE WORLD ECONOMY, RECOVERY, THE FUTURE, STOCK MARKET, WINNERS & LOSERS

Shocks have a significant impact on human development, with previous crises suggesting two patterns:

• Shocks have long-lasting consequences on human development and can be passed to subsequent generations. Even after an epidemic ends or economic growth returns, the impacts of a shock can leave lasting damage.

• The effects are unequally distributed, with vulnerable groups disproportionately affected. These patterns underscore the importance of an equity lens. As a crisis unfolds, an active approach identifying its effects and transmission mechanisms can inform timely and equitable action. It is essential to distinguish between the short-term and longer-term impacts of pandemics—and major shocks in general.

Drawing from a broad and deep historical analysis, Walter Scheidel has shown that significant shocks such as wars and pandemics can reduce income inequality but that the outcome depends on the policy response. When pandemics result in high mortality, the relative returns to labor increase compared with the returns to capital because workers demand higher compensation because there is a lower labor supply due to mortality. In part because they are afraid to be infected require more to show up for work.

In the aftermath of the Black Death in Europe during the medieval period, where the policy response accommodated these demands, income and wealth inequality fell sharply. It was repressed, as in parts of Eastern Europe, it triggered social arrangements based on serfdom that lasted for centuries and led to large and persistent wealth inequalities.

Recent analysis confirms that real wages often increase for a long time after a pandemic. But actual interest rates also decline and remain low for a long time (in part because, unlike during wars, there is no destruction of physical capital), decreasing returns to wealth and making it easier to fund public spending. It is unknown whether these historical patterns will play out in the long-run aftermath of COVID-19, in part because life expectancy now is much higher, and mortality may be lower than in previous pandemics. Moreover, interest rates are already meager in developed countries. And beyond income and wealth inequality, the implications for disparities in human development are even less clear.

To shed some light on possible implications for human development, we explore three examples of recent shocks in three different areas: the economy, health, and natural hazards. The latter two may be exacerbated or become more frequent due to climate change pressures the environment.

Economic shock: The 2008 global financial crisis

The 2008 global financial crisis, which started in the banking and financial sector, had worldwide and long-lasting impacts. International trade contracted considerably, GDP shrank, jobs disappeared, and remittances fell. The IMF documented that GDP was still below what it would have been on the pre-crisis trend ten years after the crisis. On the social side, the problem slowed progress towards the Millennium Development Goals, particularly in Sub-Saharan Africa. Some impacts of the global economic crisis were not immediately evident and are being understood only today.

After the crisis, the pace of technological adoption slowed—even more in countries with higher crisis-related output losses. This is seen in research and development spending and the adoption of industrial robots.

The crisis also affected the direction of technological change. High output-loss countries and low output-loss countries differed in the relative impacts of the displacement effects of technology on the one hand and the other's reinstatement and productivity effects. In developed economies, with large GDP losses resulting from the crisis, technology tended to replace workers, driven by industries with large shares of medium-skilled workers. But in emerging economies with lower losses, new technologies were accompanied by higher employment growth.

Global youth unemployment jumped after the crisis and has since remained high and even increasing, showing how a shock's impacts can be particularly severe for a vulnerable group.

Economic crises threaten health and health system performance. Financial pressure hinders access to health services while the need for health services grows. Adverse health effects disproportionately affect groups already vulnerable to shocks, such as unemployed people. Mental health problems also increase.

Health shock: Ebola in West Africa

During 2014–2016, West African countries faced the most significant recorded Ebola outbreak, and one that was unprecedented in which it spread in urban areas. Most of the cases came through Guinea, Liberia, and Sierra Leone, where the combined official death toll was 11,310. But that figure underestimates the human development cost of the crisis. More people are estimated to have died due to the outbreak through indirect channels than from the Ebola virus itself.

Country responses to health crises typically channel resources away from government services and primary health care. Help for a disease outbreak focus on addressing the problem: testing and then managing confirmed cases. Weak social protection and health systems that lack resilience can result in an underprovision of social care and health, which eventually can lead indirectly to deaths. Combined with this challenge is health workers' fear of getting infected during the outbreak.

The reduction in access to health care during the Ebola outbreak increased estimated deaths due to malaria, HIV/AIDS, and tuberculosis by 6,269 in Guinea, 1,535 in Liberia, and 2,819 in Sierra Leone. Decreases in vaccination rates compound these challenges. Further, the health system experienced other consequences, including the deaths of health workers.

In Sierra Leone, antenatal care coverage fell 22 percentage points, family planning six percentage points, facility delivery eight percentage points, and postnatal care services 13 percentage points during the Ebola outbreak. The reduced access to routine reproductive and maternal services translated into 3,600 additional maternal, neonatal, and stillbirth deaths in 2014–2015 under the most conservative scenario. During a health crisis, having accurate information on the outbreak is essential for indirect deaths. The indirect mortality effects of a problem with a health system that lacks resilience may be as significant as the crisis's direct mortality effects.

Natural hazard shock: Hurricane Maria

Climate change is supercharging hurricanes. In September 2017, Puerto Rico was hit by Hurricane Maria, a category five hurricane that made landfall a healthy category four storm. The official number of casualties was. But that figure—released a few days after the hurricane—accounted mostly for those who died during the event.

How many more people died in Puerto Rico as an indirect result of Maria? On 9 December 2017, the New York Times published an article asserting that the number of casualties was 1,052.68. In 2018 two academic studies estimated even higher numbers: 4,64569 and 2,975. Moving from direct death counts to more comprehensive estimates based on higher mortality following the hurricane makes a huge difference. Statistical systems often monitor only the immediate effects of shocks rather than the longer-term ones.

Social differences influence a hurricane's human impact. Maria affected all social groups but the lowest socio-economic group the most. And there is a clear divergence in how people recovered: While the medium and highest socio-economic groups showed recovery in hurricane-related mortality after two months, the lowest socioeconomic group saw estimated excess deaths related to Maria's peak four months after the hurricane.

A human development perspective on how to respond to COVID-19

The policy response to COVID-19 has to balance public health priorities with economic and social activities, accommodating short-term measures to mitigate the virus's spread and long-term effects.

The human development approach places protection and enhancing of human capabilities as the central anchor that guides the written analysis and policy, with a systemic and long-term view. The health and economic responses are to be shaped to protect and expand capabilities during and after the crisis: The health response to promote long and healthy lives, the economic reaction to accommodate a well-calibrated "downtime" with the protection of living standards.

From this perspective, there is not an intrinsic tradeoff between the health and economic dimensions. Countries and communities able to tackle health shock through nonpharmaceutical interventions are expected to be better off in the long term. Still, in a short time, nonpharmaceutical interventions lower economic activity and constrain activities for which social distance is difficult or impossible, such as education in schools. Suppose systemic mechanisms are in place, and an equity lens is applied. In that case, economic and social measures to support nonpharmaceutical interventions losses in human development can be significantly reduced in the short term and transformed into opportunities in a long time, linking (to the extent possible) immediate action with structural needs. On the other hand, nonpharmaceutical interventions lack proper implementation, focusing on preserving or expanding capabilities; there might be long-lasting well-being costs.

What would a systemic mechanism look like? Standard countercyclical economic policies that consider only the economy are not well suited to a systemic response. The more usual approach will most likely be entirely relevant in the recovery phase. But when the shock affects several dimensions simultaneously (through direct or indirect channels), balancing short-term need and longer-term impacts could be accomplished if the guiding principle for policy decisions is enhancing equity in capabilities.

Inequalities in human development represent a lack of capabilities for a large part of the population. During crises, these inequalities tend to increase, at least in the short run. The priority should be to reduce gaps by boosting the capabilities of those already falling behind before the crisis. A strategy consistent with this principle depends on the availability of resources. Without savings, insurance systems, or access to capital markets, the national and international public sectors must step in and facilitate transfers to overcome transitory shocks.

This requires assistance to those who are being asked not to work or be economically active. This section illustrates how capabilities and their distributions matter to the health and economic responses to the crisis. The support for necessary capabilities is crucial to contain the indirect adverse effects of COVID-19 on people. Enhanced capabilities—access to technology, knowledge, and quality health services—are not a luxury. They play a crucial role in dealing with the crisis, in both adaptation and mitigation.

People's capabilities and health response

People's capabilities play a vital role in response to the COVID-19 crisis. Nonpharmaceutical interventions are linked to enablers that make the intervention less costly or facilitate its success. All the interventions represent a form of social distancing that affects peoples' ability to interact with others in work, school, shopping, recreation, and social life.

The enablers might reduce the human development losses associated with COVID-19 restrictions in multiple dimensions, opening alternative capabilities: access to goods and services, access to income-generating activities, access to education, and access to social life recreation opportunities. They both increase the likelihood of the interventions' success and reduce their human development costs.

Most of the enablers are related to enhanced capabilities—the new necessities of the 21st century—which are unequally distributed across the population. As documented by the 2019 Human Development Report, gaps have been widening over the past few years.

These enhanced capabilities can reduce the impact of the downtime to overcome the health crisis caused by COVID-19. Thus, in low human development communities, nonpharmaceutical interventions will tax people's welfare more and be less effective. Forming enhanced capabilities—even during these critical times—would reduce such disparities.

The emphasis on enhanced capabilities does not mean that the work on the necessary qualifications is done. On the contrary: million people still lack access to primary sources of clean water, and around 3 billion people lack a primary handwashing facility with soap and water in their household. Failing to address necessary capabilities in responding to the COVID-19 crisis could even reverse the convergence documented in the 2019 Human Development Report.

Access to technologies

The unequal access to technologies is having a sizable effect on communities' ability to confront COVID-19. Inequality in household means and support leads to unequal experiences with online learning. The disruption in education due to COVID-19 has been unprecedented. Schools have closed nationwide in at least 147 countries, affecting more than 1.4 billion children and youth, around 86 percent of the world's student population.

This is a staggering development for school-going children, with long-term consequences for their potential. The extent to which formal schooling is substituted with learning at home—through parent involvement, own initiative, and internet availability—is a function of household means and support. As the 2019 Human Development Report indicated, parents' COVID-19 and Human Development: Assessing the Crisis, Envisioning the Recovery education shapes children's learning. In the US, children of professional parents are exposed to more than three times as many words as children in households that receive welfare benefits.

Public education should serve as an equalizer, to the extent that it can break the intergenerational transmission of inequality. Quality education, regardless of parent education background, is intended to provide equal opportunity to everyone. By disrupting schooling, the pandemic takes that away from hundreds of millions of children and makes it harder to break the intergenerational transfer of disadvantage.

In many countries, school systems and universities have moved their courses and learning online. As examined in the 2019 Human Development Report, access to technology is unequal across countries. And while there is convergence in essential technologies such as mobile phone subscriptions, digital gaps between countries and within states widen in other technologies such as access to computers, internet, and broadband—all examples of enhanced capabilities.

The interaction of the pandemic and the inequality in enhanced capabilities means that many countries lack the option to move courses and schoolwork online. If things continue, the countries left behind will also lack this option shortly (divergence). The digital gap is responsible for an excellent dispersion in effective out-of-school rates in 2020.

Even in countries that have moved to school online, not everyone has the same experience, and outcomes are mediated by inequality. In very high human development countries, there are only 28.3 subscriptions of broadband internet per 100 inhabitants. In other words, even in rich countries, not everyone has access.

CHAPTER 5
CONTROVERSY - LAB ACCIDENT FROM WUHAN, ON PURPOSE OR NOT, OTHER AGENCIES INVOLVEMENT MAYBE, CIA, CHINES SECURITY ETC.

With more than 1.4 billion children's schools closed indefinitely, new technology-based measures are in place to continue learning processes. This positive development from the recent technological revolution supports the resilience to shocks in education, a fundamental human development dimension.

So, what is the effective out-of-school rate after considering these efforts? Adjusting the percentage of primary, school-age children facing school closures to account for households with access to the Internet–and opportunity to continuing structured learning sheds some light on this question. The result represents a lower bound of the out-of-school rate—or the best performance that the school system can deliver given the structural conditions—because it assumes that every child with internet access can continue the learning process. In other words, it is an optimistic estimate of the social ability to keep children in school. It is also an optimistic estimate of inequalities between country groups because it assumes that it is equally challenging to implement these systems in every context (with high or low income, with or without broadband, with or without proper hardware).

The effective out-of-school rate has jumped substantially everywhere (even under optimistic assumptions). The sufficient out-of-school quality for primary education is highest in low human development countries (86 percent, an increase of 59 percentage points). Medium human development countries follow them (74 percent, an increase of 67 percentage points, which is the most massive reversal) and high human development countries (47 percent, an increase of 41 percentage points). Only in very high human development countries do the majority of primary-school-age children have the potential to continue structured learning, with an effective out-of-school rate of 20 percent (an increase of 19 percentage points).

Overall, this is the most massive reversal of this indicator in history, opening new human development gaps. Being out of school—even for a limited amount of time—is expected to have long-term impacts on learning, earning potential, and well-being.

This short-term analysis is based on countries experiencing school closures, which are expected to last only a few months. What happens with the global picture for 2020? Assuming that school closures stay for only one-fourth of the academic year (a conservative assumption based on the experience of several countries in Europe and North America), the annualized effective out-of-school rate for primary education for 2020 is expected to reach 20 percent.

This massive setback brings the out-of-school rate to its 1985 level. Technology's role can be assessed using two scenarios. Without internet access, the effective rate would reach 29 percent, a five-decade reversal. It is possible to evaluate the role of inequality in human development in a second scenario. If countries had the best performers' internet access rate in their human development groups, the out-of-school rate would be 12 percent.

Measures are in place to quickly bridge the divide within countries. For instance, New York City distributed 175,000 laptops, iPads, and Chromebooks before remote learning started. One internet provider has offered households with K–12 and college students free wifi access and broadband for 60 days. While developed countries are likely to start implementing some of these measures, the principles behind them should be the basis of a worldwide effort to close the gaps in technology access.

Nearly a year and a half since Covid-19 was detected in the Chinese city of Wuhan, the question of how the virus first emerged remains a mystery.

But in recent weeks the controversial claim that the pandemic might have leaked from a Chinese laboratory - once dismissed by many as a fringe conspiracy theory - has been gaining traction.

Now, US President Joe Biden has announced an urgent investigation that will look into the theory as a possible origin of the disease.

So what do we know about the competing theories - and why does the debate matter?

It's a suspicion that the coronavirus may have escaped, accidentally or otherwise, from a laboratory in the central Chinese city of Wuhan where the virus was first recorded.

Its supporters point to the presence of a major biological research facility in the city. The Wuhan Institute of Virology (WIV) has been studying coronaviruses in bats for over a decade.

The institute is a 40-minute drive from the Huanan wet market where the first cluster of infections emerged in Wuhan.

Those who support the theory say it could have leaked from a WIV lab and spread to the wet market.

Most argue it would have been an unaltered virus collected from the wild, rather than engineered.

The controversial theory first emerged early on in the pandemic, and was promoted by then-US President Donald Trump. Some even suggested it could have been engineered as a possible biological weapon.

While many in the media and politics dismissed these as conspiracy theories at the time, others called for more consideration of the possibility. Nevertheless, the idea resurfaced in recent weeks.

Safe space and balanced care work

The COVID-19 pandemic is compounding risks to further progress towards gender equality. The crisis is deepening preexisting inequalities and exposing vulnerabilities, which amplifies the impacts of the pandemic. Women and girls' impact spans the economic (earning less, saving less and job insecurity), reproductive health, unpaid care work, bargaining house power, and gender-based violence.

At the household level, gender inequalities come through a vicious cycle of powerlessness, often rooted in gender social norms that force women to face heavily restricted or even "tragic choices." Because of nonpharmaceutical interventions, many women are forced to stay home and isolate in a space that is supposed to be safe. There, they are forced to confront their households' reality, where they carry a disproportionate burden for unpaid care work and where their exposure to domestic violence increases.

Globally, women average 2.5 times as much unpaid care and domestic work as men. This affects women's labor force participation, hinders their productivity, and limits their opportunities to allocate time. And the closure of childcare and schools has had a differential effect on them since they provide most of their households' care for their children and older adults. As for other inequalities, gender inequalities in enhanced capabilities can be exacerbated by measures taken during the pandemic if households lack enablers. Under such conditions, women will see their burden increase and their effective labor participation and productivity—enhanced capabilities—constrained, limiting their opportunities to live at their full potential at work and in their households. In the United States, married women provide 60 percent of unpaid care work, even among couples who work full time. If the relative distribution of the burden remains the same and outstanding care work needs rise by 20 hours a week during the pandemic, this means 12 hours more a week for women and 8 hours more for men. Without arrangements for flexible work hours, one spouse will likely have to cease or reduce hours in paid employment temporarily. Because of the patterns in labor division, this is more likely to be the woman. Women's permanence in their households poses a challenge for their bargaining power and participation in household decision-making.

One of the cruelest forms of oppression is gender-based violence—it magnifies inequalities and reflects traditional social norms that legitimize harassment and discrimination. More than a third of women—and more than two-thirds in some countries—have experienced physical or sexual violence inflicted by a non-partner. Violence against women comes through social norms or attitudes. Globally, 30 percent of people believe it is justifiable for a man to beat his partner. These behaviors and attitudes threaten not just women but also their children, especially when women face shocks such as earthquakes, hurricanes, or health emergencies.

While it is too early for comprehensive data, there are already many profoundly concerning reports of increased violence against women worldwide. Reported cases have doubled in some countries. With preliminary evidence from Argentina, Brazil, Canada, China, Cyprus, France, Germany, Italy, Spain, and the United States—there is a consistent pattern of increased domestic violence cases reported due to COVID-19 isolation.

Underlying gender inequalities affect women's fundamental capabilities and opportunities, elevating the costs of pandemic measures. When applying nonpharmaceutical interventions, it is essential to communicate the consequences of amplifying gender inequalities in enhanced capabilities. For unpaid care work, governments can use several mechanisms to lessen the burden—for example, increasing investment in child and elder care, implementing more flexible work arrangements, or conducting media campaigns to shift traditional household norms. Staying home creates a window of opportunity to change social norms and role models, perhaps pushed by fathers more involved in unpaid care work. For gender-based violence, it is essential to make resources available to report, control, and manage cases; guarantee health services and shelters for domestic violence survivors, and ensure the continuity of judiciary services.

Inequality in public health and innovation systems

Inequality in human development affects countries' capacity to respond to COVID-19. Countries with lower human development have a fraction of developed economies' resources to support their health systems. Their health expenditure is 4.5 percent of GDP, compared with 12.1 percent for very high human development countries (with GDP per capita 15 times larger).

The availability of resources is intertwined with the ability to react to a crisis at multiple levels. First is the ability to monitor the problem for decision-making. Very few countries are conducting widespread testing, crucial for decisionmaking at the individual, community, and national levels. The logistics have proven difficult even in developed countries.

Data are unavailable for a large number of developing countries, suggesting a minimal capacity to test and implement containment measures, such as contact tracing.

The second is the ability to treat those requiring medical attention. Low human development countries have only 0.2 physicians per 1,000 people, compared with 3.1 in very high human development countries. This gap has been growing over the past decade, reflecting widening inequalities in enhanced capabilities. Similarly, the availability of hospital beds has become one of the most significant constraints for health systems. This is related not only to development gaps between countries but also to inequality within countries, particularly in weak universal health services.

The third is developing new products and services to adapt to the changing circumstances in the health system and beyond. Investment in research and development (in terms of expenditure and human resources), a proxy of innovating, is positively correlated with social development. The already large gaps have widened over the past decade.

CHAPTER 6
DIFFERENT TYPES OF IMPACT OF COVID19

There is no argument that the local economic and social spheres and global spheres have been challenged, and some sectors have been drastically dismantled. Therefore, we need to trust our trust in local spheres that facilitate our basic needs and socio-economic needs structure. As we know very well, we own a substantial service sector, rather than the industrial and agricultural sectors.

In contrast to these sectors, we need to maintain sound industrial and agricultural sectors to sustain a profitable service sector. However, the world's industrial sector will get damaged due to COVID-19. The apparel and textile industry will be heavily damaged due to COVID-19 since the pandemic has severely affected giant countries such as the USA and European countries. This will lead to lesser and lesser demand for ready-made apparel, leading to many apparel industries' closure. The factories would not be able to overcome this situation since their buyers would cut down all possible avenues to recover from the dire situation. The export volumes of the agricultural and fisheries sectors would decrease, creating negative economic and social impacts on Sri Lanka.

Though the World Bank stated on March 30, 2020, it does not provide any forecasts on Sri Lanka or South Asian countries. It focuses only on East Asian and Pacific countries while highlighting the poverty incident that would increase dramatically. If the economic situation deteriorates further and the lower-case scenario prevails, poverty is estimated to increase by about 11 million people in these regions. In April 2020, the World Bank illustrates the South Asian context of COVID-19 and its impacts. It says that the pandemic's impact will hit hard low-income people, mostly informal workers in the hospitality, retail trade, and transport sectors who have limited or no access to healthcare or social safety nets.

Furthermore, it focuses that the Sri Lankan economic growth in the first quarter of 2020 is between 3.0 and −0.5, and it will remain low throughout the year. It may slowly grow until 2022, with a 2.5% growth rate. The forecast analysis shows that Sri Lanka will struggle with the economy. Thus, the country needs a well-integrated plan to avoid economic hardships and social and political tensions. Primarily, it needs political stability, a high level of mass participation in all sectors, attitude change in domestic production and use, and a low level of dependency on foreign aids and foreign goods and services. Significantly, it will help to refurbish the domestic supply chain as the countries' primary target.

When you look at the scenario in Sri Lanka, the economic growth has translated into shared prosperity, with the national poverty headcount ratio declining from 15.3% in 2006/07 to 4.1% in 2016. Extreme poverty is rare and concentrated within some geographical pockets; however, a relatively large population subsists slightly more than the poverty line. However, COVID-19 would increase poverty incidents since many apparel sector workers are unemployed or underemployed. Foreign migrant laborers are affected due to the situations in their respective countries and are losing their decent income. Simultaneously, the tourism and hotel industry will be severely affected, sometimes temporarily, as Sri Lanka manages the pandemic situation satisfactorily, attracting future foreign tourists on the lookout for healthy living. SuppoSuppose the Government of Sri Lanka (GOSL) plans a well-integrated domestic production, strengthening, and improvement activities. In that case, it will ensure the flow of the national supply chain without any disturbances. Also, such a situation may help to gain significant advances in local and foreign tourism.

Within the socio-economic background highlighted above, Sri Lanka needs to have a comprehensive future action plan to overcome all negative impacts. It is essential to identify the short-term, medium-term, and long-term negative and positive effects in developing a future action plan or COVID-19 recovery action plan.

When focusing on positive impacts, the immediate question that may arise is the positive implications in a global pandemic situation? Socially, there is a non-practical perspective and a method called functionalism or functional perspective, and this method could be utilized in analyzing the impact of social action. COVID-19 is a social action, and it can also be considered a significant social problem based on Richard Puller's definition. When looked at generally, COVID-19 is a disease spreading through close human contacts in day-to-day social relationships. It is a virus, and individual sections also consider this to be a human-made virus or biological weapon. There is no conclusive evidence on who made it or for what purpose. The majority of those directly affected are the elderly, and a considerable number of people are dying. The percentage is changing from country to country. Therefore, the USA, which is highly affected, shows that 2.9% of the deaths are amongst these affected persons.

The death toll is very high in Italy, which is 13%. In Sri Lanka, it is 3.7%, and it is a higher figure compared to India, which is 2.8%. Thus, it is essential to understand what the positive impacts are. They are given in the following:

1. People adapt to a pandemic situation, and they also understand what the ideal social behavior is in a similar condition. This may include government pandemic management systems and policies.

2. They learned about social distancing and its rules, conditions, and procedures. Especially how painful it is but useful within the family and the community. Also, they adapt themselves to the situation while contemplating the difference between a usual case and a pandemic situation.

3. As a result of social integration, families, and communities engage in a high social cohesion or social conscience to face difficult situations. Hence, everyone is getting used to an everyday lifestyle, sharing and caring for others, especially older people.

4. The death of an elderly or chronically ill person results in a reorganization or reunion of the family unit. Though it is not easy to bear the psycho-social factors, they finally come to certain common conclusions.

5. Similarly, the government and regional organizations in the global context may reunite to face the pandemic situation—for example, the SARRC countries reunited over COVID-19 and set up financial allocations for supporting poorer nations. The recent SAARC video conference on COVID 19 has resulted in establishing a fund for regional cooperation to combat the pandemic. India's giant country contributed USD 10 million, followed by Sri Lanka, which contributed USD 5 to the fund. It is possible to utilize this fund to improve

domestic and regional production while aiming at an uninterrupted supply chain in the agricultural, industrial, and service sectors.

6. Medical systems in any country will be improved to sustainable levels to face a pandemic situation. They will understand the existing gaps in these systems. Many South and East Asian countries will mainly focus on their indigenous medical systems. Journal of Social and Economic Development and its integration with the biomedical system shows more unsatisfactory results. Indigenous medical practitioners may challenge Their dominant authority due to the indigenous medical systems' strength to treat COVID-19 patients.

7. The global hegemonic power would change, and a new hegemonic power relation is taking its place without any brutal war conditions and much economic and social costs. It seems that the USA may lose the hegemonic power, which would be replaced by China, and within such a scenario, China could achieve its long-term goals. However, it can be delayed and disturbed by the USA through certain economic restrictions against China. Recently, the USA announced that they are willing to withdraw their investments in China. Under such circumstances, South Asian countries, particularly India, can offer much better economic policies to attract US investments in India. Similarly, Sri Lanka and Bangladesh can grab some such opportunities in specific industrial fields. This may help in improving supply chain values and efficiency in South Asian countries.

8. The new hegemonic power may extend its supporting hands to the developing nations and poorer countries. Thus, there will be a

competition amongst China, the USA, and India to support regional governments in South East Asia. The new world order may be a novel experience for the countries and their people. In the beginning, it will be optimistic as per the conflict theory in sociology. If it suits the supply chain system in these countries, they may accept the new order.

9. There will be many discoveries and innovations in all affected sectors or spheres at national, regional, and global contexts. Most of these would be medical, environment, industry, and socio-cultural related. These discoveries and innovations will help to manage the supply chain in South Asian countries.

10. The potentials would be domestic products and services to maintain local traditional lifestyles rather than modernity. People may repose their trust in many local-level trades and business firms rather than supermarket systems. These trends strengthen the supply chain network at national and regional levels. Perhaps, there may be some new trading opportunities too amongst regional countries.

11. Domestic production could increase due to family or cottage level agricultural practices, including other small-scale handicraft productions in society. This may reduce the market demand to some extent, causing adverse effects amongst international trades.

12. As mentioned above, the pandemic situation may increase the level of innovations amongst the people. Some creative-minded people may introduce many useful and productive primary and secondary things, efficient ways and means of productions, low-cost productions, technological advancements, etc. These trends, too, may strengthen the supply chain network at national and regional levels.

13. People may be attracted to traditional foods and consumption practices, mainly based on the human family. Intergenerational social integrity will strengthen and be consolidated by youths. There will be a lesser demand for restaurants and hotel sector supply chains in each level, such as national, regional, and global, due to the social and physical distancing.

14. Decline in defense expenditure at national and global levels and minimizing the need or requirements in the arms race, especially in nuclear weaponry systems, at least temporarily. Thus, war fear could be minimized in certain regions. This may, in turn, influence international terrorism and its supply chain networks.

15. New ideological constructions in many critical subject disciplines, such as medicine, economics, political science, sociology, psychology, robotic sciences, religious and Journal of Social and Economic Development humanistic sciences. Hence, research and development activities will expand in every country.

16. Developments in sociological tool-kits and social engineering skills to deliver efficient services through supply chain networks and patients and general public management.

17. People are getting used to do some optional analysis and adapt to follow the optimum use of resources, economizing resources, and sustainable approaches to satisfy their need structure. These trends may reorganize the supply chain networks at national and regional levels.

18. General public may develop some positive altitudes over the special duties performed by various essential services in society, especially health workers, social workers, police and armed forces involved in quarantine processes, etc. However, there should be very efficient supply chains to maintain these optimum operation services when necessary to society, particularly in South Asia.

19. Reduction in plastic and polythene use at the domestic level, thus reducing environmental pollution. As a whole, it may contribute to global environmental protection efforts. It may temporarily reduce greenhouse gases due to the minimum use of vehicles and industries globally. Perhaps, there may be some climate changes in the environment.

20. Reduction in environmental pollution in the world, regional and national contexts. Mainly, air, sound, and water pollution will be reduced. Some studies have been conducted, and they reveal that the pollution level is decreased drastically in all these three sectors.

21. Possible formation of other philanthropic ideas amongst the upper hierarchy segments in society. Thus, the domestic supply chain networks should capture these demands effectively.

22. If the government successfully manages the COVID-19 instead of developing a pandemic situation, it can lead to a stable political order in society. Perhaps, the incumbent government could win another term in power as the pandemic situation has provided an excellent opportunity to compare each country and its skills in their political regimes' governance.

23. Reduction in crimes such as drug addiction, alcoholism, gambling, prostitution or commercial sex, violence, and suicide. Again, the supply chain networks in commercial sex, illicit drugs, etc., may change.

24. Some countries may amend or introduce specific legislation based on their experiences in managing COVID-19 pandemic situations. Notably, trading pacts amongst regional countries may change while new alliances may also be formulated.

25. Some countries may review policy gaps and take action for policy updates. Sri Lanka needs a policy on indigenous medicine (traditional medicine), which is not covered by the existing health policy in Sri Lanka. It is the right time to respond to the court decision and request a new pharmacopeia with a list of codes.

26. More utilization of the internet for sharing ideas, new knowledge, filtering knowledge gaps, news messages, etc. This may open up more avenues to reduce the stress level of the people.

27. Return migrants who have substantial fnancial resources may invest in Sri Lanka if the socio-economic and political stability is established after complete control and management of COVID-19 in Sri Lanka.

28. Returning migrants with less or insufficient financial resources may seek jobs in the apparel or plantation sectors. Therefore, there will be a high supply in the labor market Journal of Social and Economic Development. This situation may impact the new formation of production and supply chain networks.

29. There will be more research on COVID-19, particularly discovering a vaccine and medical strategies that are more effective for inpatient management. If any new vaccinations are found, a massive demand from each country and new supply chain networks will emerge within the health sector.

Therefore, positive impacts are relatively high, and some consequences are short term, and most others are long term. This situation depends on the early stage of April 2020, and the shape could change due to several global socio-economic and political factors. So far, COVID-19 is in a rapid spread tendency in most countries. There are no good health and socio-economic facilities, mainly supply chain networks, to address the need structure of the pandemic situation in these countries. When the Indian scenario is analyzed, the COVID19 impacts will be the most painful when compared to other countries. The social system prevailing in India is not simple in terms of managing the pandemic situation. Any society which has a high social disparity may have to face the most negative impacts.

The negative impacts towards the family, communities, nations, regions, and the world push them backward in any sector or socio-economic and political spheres. Several elements which cause negative impacts can be identified as illnesses or COVID-19, pandemic situation, deaths, social distancing, curfew, and the lock-down of the entire functional mechanism of a single society and the global network in production, trade, supply chain networks, transportation, social networking, and political network. Therefore, this paper has given equal attention to the negative impacts of COVID-19 in the local, regional, and global contexts based on the situation in early April 2020. They are shown in the following:

1. The pandemic situation has spread as a global pandemic disease, which is creating fear, stress, stigma, minimizing social networks, etc.

2. Health and medical systems, especially biomedical systems, have taken their maximum effort, but the healthcare system itself is affected due to various conditions. Thus, there are many deaths reported though the biomedical system has made an enormous effort.

3. High rate of deaths due to various illnesses or complications of diseases occurring amongst the patients, especially the elderly, affected by COVID-19.

4. Impossible tasks and challenges to the medical staff, supporting staff, social workers, and health administrators at local, domestic, and global levels. The World Health Organisation (WHO) is the primary entity, followed by other United Nations (UN) agencies responsible for a regional and global pandemic situation.

5. Some countries such as Italy, Spain, the USA and China, and a few other European countries face a much higher disintegration in all subsystems of society. Thus, the social system needs a complete reorganization and integration to survive.

6. Dismantling the family relationship and intimate relationships with relatives, neighbors, various communities, etc. These conditions may lead to interpersonal conflicts and domestic violence in the family.

7. Losing the knowledge, experience, and services of the elderly would mean that the next generation would not share them for their betterment.

8. Downward trends of family economic conditions and several lower hierarchy social classes facing unbearable financial hardships due to lack of daily or monthly earnings. Though there are market accessibility and supply chain network even under social mobility limitation, they do not possess the purchasing power.

9. Disruptions of schools, universities, and vocational education segments where they have to seek specific optional strategies to cover their educational goals. Primarily, they may face some irreversible gaps in their education. All supply chain networks in the education field have been interrupted.

10. Some people may face various kinds of stress, social stigma, and depression conditions due to the social system's malfunction.

11. Possible social conflicts or conflicts of interests in the subsystems may lead to the social system. Some institutions and organizations may not possess sufficient capacities to find remedial solutions to fill the gaps and issues.

12. Decline in religious belief systems and practices in all religions, and people may not believe in superstitious powers, in god, and other divine and invisible elements in society.

13. If the government and its subordinate authorities face some bad workable decisions or binding decisions and low policy applications, it may lead to political instability in society. These conflicts of interest may cause political changes in society.

14. Social unrest, stress, and social stigma amongst the family members due to their detachment from family due to local and international migration. This may get aggravated further through the suspension of continental air transportation under lock-down situations.

15. Disruptions in the productions of primary and secondary items in society. Mainly, issues in the production of direct items may lead to social unrest in society. Less demand and lack of good supply chain networks may aggravate the current unrest level.

16. Many people are losing their jobs and incomes in the formal and informal sectors of society.

17. Service providers' (supply chain networks) inability to continue the day-to-day supply of commodities and other services due to the lack of profit margins. It may lead to detachments from such entities or services, and some people may find alternative solutions. Thus, there may be some temporal decline in supply chains in society.

18. People might depend on rumors and other informal channels of information if there

is a chaotic condition of information channels or disseminating information. If there are some loop halls in supply chain networks, they may work rapidly with different social and economic impacts.

19. Certain social classes may display their egoistic ideologies when accumulating primary or essential goods and services. This may cause some negative attitudes amongst other social studies by creating a conflict of interest.

20. Global economic recession and increase in poverty level in society. This may lead to financial crises such as a decline in monetary values, share market values and businesses, changes in supply chain networks, and people's purchasing power.

21. The country has to take alternative action to maintain a stable economy. The developing countries and developing countries may get more loans and grants for their economy to survive. Thus, there will be a more economic and political dependency in these countries. As a result of this condition, countries in the hegemonic circle may directly or indirectly fulfill their hidden agendas in such dependent countries' territories. Being South Asian countries, there are specific common social and economic characteristics that need to be safeguarded during the pandemic situation.

22. The pandemic situation will directly influence the Sustainable Development Goals (SDGs) defined to be achieved by 2030 since some countries may not allocate financial resources to meet the country-specific targets.

23. Internal fragmentation may occur in global hegemonic countries, particularly in the USA, and they may attempt to regain the hegemonic power through various economic and political strategies. Perhaps, they may go for direct war strategies with other countries or accelerate existing intervention in the Middle-East region.

24. Sri Lankans who have been employed in foreign countries may return home, and future foreign revenues may reduce. One of the significant revenue in Sri Lanka, especially the migrant workers in the Middle-East, Europe, and East Asian countries, made a substantial contribution to the Sri Lankan economy. This may cause some effects in supply chain networks in Sri Lanka as well as South Asian countries.

25. If the government of Sri Lanka does not engage the returning migrants fruitfully, they may get frustrated and thus cause some vulnerability in the informal sectors of society.

When these positive and negative impacts are considered, it is evident that COVID19 has caused more positive effects on the nations, regions and the world, mainly South Asian countries. However, some countries such as Italy, Spain, the USA, and China, and several European countries have suffered much. When writing this article, COVID-19 had infected 5,306,928 persons worldwide (when the report was finalized for publication, the number has increased up to 15,947,291). Comparatively, these positive and negative impacts are valid for these countries, too, irrespectively of the spread of COVID-19.

The proposed future action plan or COVID-19 recovery action plan mainly focuses on the socio-economic, environmental, and political spheres and not on the medical and technical spheres.

When these different domains or spheres are looked at, it becomes evident that there are higher numbers of actions identified under social environments. It implies that COVID-19 is a pandemic situation. It has more critical aspects in the social domain that needs to be looked at through a sociological rather than administrative or political perspective.

Furthermore, all responsible officers and the public could provide at least a minimum input than all actions highlighted in Table 1. Moreover, most of the proposed measures are focused on short-term and medium-term actions. However, some significant activities identified under long-term actions related to individual and group level attitudes.

All these analyses were done and elaborated in different subsections of the paper, highlight a pivotal role in the supply chain networks and management clusters in every society. In South Asian countries, supply chain networks and management are more specific than in other parts of the world because they maintain a dual-mode of the economy—subsistence and commercial. Mainly, end-users and consumers are engaged in some domestic or cottage production systems. If they have a surplus, then they share it with their relatives and neighbors as a cultural habit. Thus, they are not dependent on the market system. Some of them sell these domestic products to boutiques. Sometimes they give some value addition as cottage products and try to sustain a stable supply chain network. This situation is seen in many South Asian countries.

Therefore, sustainability in supply chain networks in South Asian countries is highly volatile. However, it is evident that the supply chain networks are influential and of paramount importance under the COVID 19 pandemic situation in South Asian countries.

Tourism facing an unprecedented challenge

In an unprecedented crisis to the tourism sector, possible scenarios point to declines of 60% to 80% in international tourist arrivals for the year, depending on the containment speed and the duration of travel restrictions and shutdown of borders. Additionally, there will be an impact on the availability of tourism-related statistical data for 2020

Closure of borders travels bans and quarantine measures in many countries directly affecting the tourism sector like no other. After increasing almost uninterruptedly and more than doubling since 2000, UNWTO expects international arrivals in 2020 to decrease by 60 to 80 percent concerning 2019, depending on when travel restrictions are lifted. Available data show that March's month's arrivals dropped by 60 percent concerning the same month in 2019.

Many of the country's most significantly affected by the health emergency are vital players in the global tourism ecosystem, either as destinations, source markets, or both. States with the highest number of reported cases account for about 55 and 68 percent of global inbound and outbound tourism expenditure, respectively. The effects of the crisis on these economies will spill out to other countries, and the impact will be particularly critical on territories that are heavily dependent on international tourism.

These developing economies are thus more vulnerable to the impact of COVID-19, as they depend significantly on inbound tourism, especially from those countries that at the moment are most directly affected by the pandemic. The current situation also affects the data needs and the capacity to deliver in the crisis's aftermath. While countries are making great efforts in filling the data gaps, the continuity of essential sources can be affected, including household, border, and accommodation establishments surveys. In this context, those affected countries need to explore alternative data sources and collaborate with industry data partners to fill the gaps.

Disruption of the international postal supply chain

Postal operators worldwide have been facing hurdles in providing their traditional services due to the COVID-19 outbreak. In particular, governments' sanitary measures have restricted access to labor (e.g., social distancing) and transportation services (e.g., closure of airports). Simultaneously, in countries experiencing significant economic shutdowns, postal services have been deemed vital and continue to function in contrast to many other businesses.

As the UN agency in charge of coordinating cross-border postal activity, the Universal Postal Union (UPU) monitors international mail in real-time through its big data platform. Through its Emergency

Information System (EmIS), it also collects essential information on postal operators' capacity to supply services.

As of April 20, 2020, 124 countries have submitted EmIS messages to announce disruptions in their operations. The international transport capacity has been the most impacted area, with over 170 EmIS messages sent to the UPU since the crisis. The disruption of air-routes has eventually impacted the delivery of many postal items.

By calculating the ratio between items ready to be exported and items received by the importing country, one can measure the level of disruption in the international supply chain. The rate is slightly above one in regular times, as in a given week, the importing country receives almost every exported item. Since February 2020, the percentage has climbed, and as of April 2020, for every 1.8 weekly item shipped, only one is notified as received.

Problems related to the availability of labor (69 EmIS announcements) have also lengthened the clearance of items through customs, with bar-coded parcels showing an increase from an average of 2 hours to over 64 hours.

CHAPTER 7
IMPACT OF COVID-19 IN AFRICA

It is too early to know the full impact of COVID-19 on Africa. To date, the experience has been varied. There are causes for concern, but also reasons for hope. Early estimates were pessimistic regarding the pandemic's impact on the continent. But the relatively low numbers of COVID-19 cases reported thus far have raised hopes that African countries may be spared the worst of the pandemic. While the virus is present in all African countries, most countries have recorded fewer than 1,000 cases. The African Union acted swiftly, endorsing a joint continental strategy in February, and complementing efforts by Member States and Regional Economic Communities by providing a public health platform. Caution is warranted, however, as these are early days in the life cycle of a disease that is still not fully understood and where we have seen repeated patterns of first slow, then exponential growth in the number of cases. The low numbers recorded so far could be linked to minimal capacities for testing and reporting cases. WHO has warned that the pandemic could kill between 83,000 and 190,000 people in 47 African countries in the first year, mostly depending on governments' responses. The socio-economic impacts could "smolder" for several years.

Moreover, as with other regions, there is not one homogenous narrative around the COVID-19 pandemic in Africa. The pandemic is affecting African countries differently, given varied strengths and vulnerabilities. Only one-third of Africans have access to proper handwashing, for instance, and there is less than one doctor per one thousand people on the continent.1 But some countries also have a wealth of relevant lessons from dealing with previous HIV/AIDS and Ebola epidemics on engaging communities, communicating risks, and adapting local and innovative methods to craft African approaches to control the spread of the disease.

The Africa Centres for Disease Control and Prevention boosts the region's capacities by building testing capabilities, promoting knowledge-based pandemic management, and supporting governments' efforts to mobilize resources for a sustained health response. While the immediate health impact is still evolving, the indirect consequences beyond health already bring a heavy toll. These include food insecurity, lack of medical supplies, loss of income and livelihood, difficulties in applying sanitary and physical distancing measures, a looming debt crisis, and related political and security risks. This policy brief takes a snapshot of the pandemic's immediate impacts on health, economies, peace, safety, human rights, and humanitarian assistance in Africa. It outlines response measures currently being taken by African and external stakeholders. It provides recommendations to protect gains in the fight against the pandemic and maximize opportunities to recover for a more inclusive and sustainable future as countries emerge from this crisis.

KEY FINDINGS EMERGE FROM ANALYSIS:

HEALTH:

The global health response must emphasize solidarity towards developing countries, guided by health as a global public good. African countries, with partner support, can take measures to improve testing capacities, access to medical supplies, and participation in vaccine and treatment research; enhance production and innovation through intra-African collaboration; expand deployment of community health workers, which proved useful during previous health crises; and boost medical personnel capacity, including by tapping into diaspora expertise. Once vaccines or medical treatment for COVID-19 are discovered, Africa must benefit from equal access. These measures must also be part of a comprehensive effort to improve the resilience and preparedness of healthcare systems that will be increasingly exposed to risks, from climate-induced natural disasters to conflicts.

SOCIO-ECONOMIC:

To help address this crisis's devastating economic and social consequences, we need a comprehensive global response package amounting to a double-digit percentage of global Gross Domestic

Product. For Africa, that means more than $200 billion. All of Africa's partners must mobilize. We also need an across-the-board debt standstill for African countries and comprehensive debt sustainability and solutions for structural issues in the international debt architecture. Increased resources from the multilateral lending agencies, including raising IMF Special Drawing Rights, will also be critical to the region's success in dealing with the pandemic's consequences. Measures to address the crisis's economic and social fall-out must include direct support that will keep households afloat and businesses solvent. There must be a focus on the most affected. African governments so far took steps to save lives and protect livelihoods with a "people first" approach, and their efforts to support large, medium, and small enterprises, as well as the informal sector, which is the predominant sector for women's employment, need to be scaled up substantially, supported by all partners. Emergency budgetary support is also required to procure essential lifesaving materials and effect the immediate socio-economic response.

FOOD SECURITY:

Many Africans risk becoming food insecure as a consequence of this crisis. It is essential to prioritize agriculture by declaring it a critical sector that should not be interrupted by COVID-19 related measures. Food corridors need to be secured, and farmers supported to ensure uninterrupted supplies and food security. Similarly, the focus should be on regions and communities where risks are most acute, strengthening social protection systems and safeguarding access to food and nutrition for the most vulnerable groups, especially young children, pregnant and breastfeeding women, older people, and other at-risk groups.

PEACE AND SECURITY:

While dealing with the menace of the pandemic, maintaining peace and security in Africa remains paramount. In this regard, priorities include silencing the guns, implementing the Secretary-General's and the African Union Commission Chairperson's appeal for a ceasefire, sustaining peace processes and critical peace operations. The response to COVID-19 needs to be "conflict-sensitive" and avoid generating new tensions. Decisions regarding planned national elections should be taken in an inclusive and consultative manner. An inclusive security approach would also ensure that the spike in violence in the home and harmful practices, such as child marriage, and sexual abuse resulting from the pandemic, are integrated through preventive measures into all response planning.

HUMAN RIGHTS:

Keeping human rights considerations to the fore of the COVID-19 response results in better outcomes. Citizen trust in institutions, transparency, and social cohesion appears to enhance compliance with response measures. Inclusion and participation of women and youth and respect for human rights need to be upheld in delivering COVID-19-related services and in the fight against the virus. Recovery from the crisis must lead to more equal, inclusive, and sustainable economies and societies.

The View From Africa

The COVID-19 pandemic arrived at a moment when prospects for many African countries were promising. At the beginning of 2020, Africa was on track to continue its economic expansion, with growth projected to rise from 2.9 percent in 2019 to 3.2 percent in 2020 and 3.5 percent in 2021. Essential gains were being registered in poverty reduction and health indicators. Technology and innovation were being increasingly embraced across the continent, with young Africans acting as early adopters of new mobile money platforms. Progress had also been made concerning political unity and economic integration. The entry into force of the African Continental Free Trade Area (AfCFTA) in May 2019 promised to boost intra-African trade by as much as 25 percent by 2040.

Furthermore, Africa enjoyed some of the highest global returns on foreign direct investment (FDI). Several inclusive elections, increasingly the norm for most African countries, were due to be held in 2020. At the same time, as with other regions of the world, Africa faced fundamental challenges. It was not on track to achieve the goals of the 2030 Agenda and Agenda 2063.

Weak governance, corruption, environmental degradation, human rights violations, lack of economic diversity, and humanitarian and conflict situations, among others, further undermined progress. It is against this backdrop that African countries are dealing with the

COVID-19 pandemic. While the pandemic's full impact has yet to be felt, the prolonged lack of investment in critical health systems and decades of economic growth exacerbated grievances and inequality and increased Africa's vulnerability. If not controlled early, the pandemic could quickly morph into a humanitarian, socioeconomic, development, and political crises, with profoundly digitalization effects.

The news of the first Covid19 case in Africa came on 14 February 2020. By 13 May, patients had been reported in all 54 countries. The African Union acted swiftly, endorsing a joint continental strategy in February, and complementing efforts by Member States and Regional Economic Communities by providing a public health platform.

The African Union Chairperson, President Cyril Ramaphosa of South Africa, appointed four Special Envoys to mobilize international support for Africa's efforts to address the economic fallout of COVID-19. The Africa Centres for Disease Control and Prevention (Africa CDC), established in 2017, is curating real-time information and collaborates with the World Health Organization (WHO). The Africa CDC's new Partnership on Accelerated COVID-19 Testing (PACT), which aims to test 10 million people within six months, will complement government efforts while building significant inroads into promoting knowledge-based pandemic management. WHO support for a considerable ramp-up to achieve this target will be vital, given that, to date, there is limited availability of test kits across the continent. The Africa CDC has also established the Africa COVID-19 Response Fund, in collaboration with the public-private AfroChampions initiative, to raise an initial $150 million for immediate needs and up to $400 million to support a sustained health response and socio-economic assistance to the most vulnerable populations in Africa.

Most African countries moved swiftly, enforcing quarantines, lockdowns, and border closures. So far, countries with higher testing levels have experienced lower infection rates, but limited capacity has rendered it difficult to discern accurate transmission, hospitalization, and mortality rates. Regional Economic Communities have also been proactive, unveiling initiatives within their respective regions. African countries are also addressing the economic and humanitarian fallout of the pandemic. Many have already announced remedial fiscal and monetary measures and food distribution and financial support to the most vulnerable groups. More is needed in terms of immediate and direct assistance to cushion against lost income and export earnings, dwindling remittances, and decreased government revenue. However, relatively few countries have articulated initiatives to mitigate the socio-economic impacts of COVID-19.

African countries have primarily taken a middle-of-the-road approach to prevention, maintaining some level of economic activity. For example, Ghana opted for a partial lockdown for a limited period and enforced close monitoring of people's movements, providing sanitary facilities and free water to the most vulnerable. Botswana has focused on boosting the livelihoods of vulnerable households by buying food from local communities. The relative effectiveness of the different strategies across the region will only be known in time. With digitalization already transforming Africa's economies in fundamental ways, most African countries have also actively employed digital technologies to shift to cashless transactions, for example, through the use of mobile money in East Africa, which has helped reduce the risk of the spread.

In Ethiopia and Senegal, tech startups are using 3D printing to develop face shields and ventilator valves. South Africa is using cell phones for contact tracing, as opportunities for telehealth also open up. Also, African civil society actors and the private sector are forming unprecedented partnerships to fight the disease. In Nigeria, the Coalition Against COVID-19 has brought together local banks to mobilize resources to support social protection and PPE purchase. The African Influencers for Development initiative, supported by UNDP, has rallied medical professionals, finance, logistics, production, and more. Tech volunteers from the Ethiopian diaspora work with the government to develop contact tracing tools, information campaigns, and data collection tools. African sovereign wealth and pension fund leaders have announced a collaboration on supply chain and trade support through digitization, especially in healthcare and agriculture.

Ethiopian Airlines has refurbished 31 ventilators for the Ministry of Health and is set to launch ventilators with foreign partners. UN "Solidarity Flights," led by WHO, the World Food Programme (WFP), the African Union, and Africa CDC, deliver urgently needed medical equipment to all African nations in the fight against COVID-19.

Impact On Public Health

Approximately 600 million Africans (43.6 percent) live in urban areas, of which 56 percent live in slums. Many African urban households live in a single room (71 percent in Kampala), do not have potable water (80 percent in Lagos), or reside in over-crowded neighborhoods (density in Johannesburg is 9,000 per sq km). Only 34 percent of the African population has access to handwashing facilities.15 Weak health systems and the prevalence of underlying health conditions, such as HIV/ AIDS, tuberculosis, malaria, and malnutrition, as well as challenges to state authority from armed groups, render parts of the continent particularly susceptible to contagion. The pandemic has further exacerbated existing gender inequalities resulting in women having even more limited access to critical health services, systems, and information. Africa, which has 16 percent of the global population and 26 percent of the worldwide disease burden, accounted for less than 2 percent of the nearly $9.7 trillion spent globally on health in 2015. Health systems are likely to be overwhelmed by a rapid spread of the disease. Many African countries lack physicians (0.2 per 1,000 people), hospital beds (1.8 per 1,000), and the necessary health infrastructure to adequately respond to the pandemic. Twenty-three African countries, in particular, may face a too high risk of COVID-19 mortality due to a lack of hospital beds (less than 2 per 1,000 persons) and high rates of deaths from infectious and respiratory diseases (3-8 deaths per 1,000 people). As the pandemic exacerbates the burden on already weak health systems in Africa, there is a vital need to ensure that existing health services are protected, not just repurposed, for COVID-19.

Limited access to COVID 19-related supplies and equipment, such as test kits, PPE, ventilators, and pharmaceuticals, can overwhelm health systems. Disruptions in global supply chains and import tariffs are a threat since most African countries are dependent on the outside world for the majority (94 percent) of the continent's pharmaceutical needs.

As of 24 April, 80 nations had imposed restrictions on the export essential COVID-medical equipment and supplies (ventilators, PPE). Efforts are underway to convert existing manufacturing capacities to produce the crucial kit. Nurturing African productive abilities is necessary to ensure that innovations during COVID-19 outlive the pandemic, laying the groundwork for future preparedness and more diversified and expanded economic activity. Reliable energy access is vital for medical service delivery, including lighting, refrigeration, and sterilization. During the COVID-19 crisis, decentralized renewable energy solutions have been proven to be sustainable, clean, and reliable ways to power isolation centers and health facilities in Africa.

Economic Impact

The COVID-19 pandemic began to impact African economies heavily and destroy livelihoods well before it reached the continent's shores. Among the factors were: falling demand for Africa's commodities; capital flight from Africa; a virtual collapse of tourism and air transport associated with lockdowns and border closures; and depreciation of local currencies resulting from a deterioration in the current account balance. African countries cannot afford to wait until the virus is contained before implementing socio-economic support programs. Africa's significant informal sector workers (85.8 percent of the workforce) cannot comply with social distancing and stay-at-home orders without severe consequences for their lives and livelihoods. Many household earners would be forced to choose between the virus and putting food on the table.

Additionally, almost 90% of women in Africa work in the informal sector, with no social protections. Female-headed households are, particularly at risk. The July 2020 start date of trade under the AfCFTA has been postponed due to the pandemic, delaying the promise of opportunities for new exports, jobs, investments in infrastructure, and financing for Africa's development. While negotiations for the AfCFTA are on hold, there is an opportunity for African countries to assess the potential impact of a prolonged delay and to lay the technical ground for its implementation. As elsewhere globally, the African airline industry, which supports 6.2 million people, and tourism, which accounts for a significant share of the GDP, in particular, of Small Island Developing States (SIDS), have been severely disrupted. The resulting financing challenges will likely spill over to the rest of the economy as the risk of Non-Performing Loans rise. This has been a hugely disruptive impact of the crisis on tourism and the African airline industry and a blow to the institutional infrastructure that connects the continent, built over the past two decades.

Governments, shareholders, and IFIs could explore how to ensure sustainability and liquidity in these sectors, including loan guarantees and a temporary waiver of taxes. Remittances, a vital income source or supplement for numerous households in Africa, are projected to decline with a massive impact on countries such as Comoros, the Gambia, Lesotho, Liberia, and Somalia inflows account for more than 10 percent of GDP. The World Bank estimates that sub-Saharan African countries will see remittance flows drop by 23.1 percent (US$37 billion in 2020). In Somalia, remittances, which amount to US$1.4bn per year26 and comprise the largest single category of external financial support, have declined sharply. Sub-Saharan Africa currently has among the highest remittance fees, averaging 9.1 percent per transaction. The combined effect of the crisis has led to exchange rate depreciation and a projected decline in Africa's GDP. The UN Economic Commission for Africa (ECA) projects a 1.1 percent growth rate in 2020 in the best-case scenario and a contraction of -2.6 percent in the worst case, depriving 19 million people of their livelihoods and, in the context of weak social protection programs in Africa, pushing up to 29 million more people into poverty. Oil exporting nations could lose up to US$ 65 billion in revenues as crude oil prices continue to tumble.

DEBT BURDEN — UNPRECEDENTED FISCAL DEFICITS AMIDST ALREADY CONSTRAINED BUDGETS

In Africa, the average debt-to-GDP ratio had increased from 39.5 percent in 2011 to 61.3 percent in 2019. Heavy debt burdens are partly due to commercial borrowing to finance the continent's sizeable annual infrastructure financing gap of US$68 billion to US$108 billion — equivalent to about 3 to 5 percent of the continent's GDP.27 Also, most African countries lack the fiscal space to respond adequately to the crisis due to low domestic saving rates; low levels of domestic resource mobilization; high illicit financial outflows; capital flight; volatile commodity prices; high fiscal deficits, and stagnating development assistance (ODA) and FDI flows.

African Ministers of Finance and the African Union have called on development partners to provide US$100 billion, including US$44 billion in debt relief to support health systems, safeguard jobs and provide safety nets for vulnerable groups. The United Nations Secretary-General has called for more than $200 billion for Africa as part of a comprehensive global response package and an across-the-board debt standstill, options towards debt sustainability, and solutions for structural issues international debt architecture. Official creditors have mobilized up to US$57 billion for Africa so far, including about US$18 billion each from the IMF and the World Bank.30 Private creditor support in 2020 could amount to an estimated US$13 billion. Further, the G20 countries have decided to suspend debt repayment for low-income countries from 1 May 2020 to the end of the year. The IMF has also provided debt relief for 19 African countries. Furthermore, individual countries, such as the EU Member States, the US, and China, have offered support either to particular countries or to the continent. This support is crucial, but considerable additional measures, including creditors commensurate with the exceptional nature of the crisis, will be necessary.

A FOOD CRISIS

It is becoming clear that one near-term impact of this pandemic will be a dramatic rise in food insecurity and potentially devastating disruptions to the global food supply chain. Africa is likely to be deeply impacted. Despite its agricultural resources, Africa is a net importer of agricultural and food products, with ten essential foods making up 66 percent (US$46 billion) of total African food imports. If unchecked, the current economic crisis is likely to escalate to a severe food crisis, with potential peace and security implications. Several major staple crop exporters have imposed export restrictions on rice and wheat. These measures could heighten food insecurity in

Africa and result in a sharp rise in food prices and rising hunger and malnutrition. Every percentage point drop in global GDP is expected to result in an additional 0.7 million stunted children. Along with the pandemic, the second wave of desert locusts is threatening East Africa with estimates that it will be 20 times worse than the February wave that hit eight countries in the region and was the worst outbreak in 70 years. Together, they present an alarming threat to food security and livelihoods in the Horn of Africa.

EDUCATION

Prolonged school closures at all levels, combined with wide-spread economic hardship, risk undermining aspirations and potentials and widening inequalities. In sub-Saharan Africa, close to 90 percent of students do not have access to household computers, and 82 percent cannot get online. School closures have left over 330 million learners of all levels and over 8.5 million teachers unable to learn or teach from home. While mobile phones can support young learners, around 56 million live in areas that are not served by mobile networks, and access numbers are consistently worse for girls and women. Even where computers are provided, unreliable power supply and a poor internet connection, coupled with financial costs, undermine such investments. Increased internet reach can lessen the gap in education access through continued learning and provide a vital source of information and awareness about the pandemic.

Peace and security impacts

To date, many African countries have managed the political risks associated with the measures to respond to the pandemic. Opposition to lockdowns and other restrictive measures has been sporadic and political tensions surrounding elections have been mostly kept in check. In some countries, the COVID-19 context strengthened political dialogue among national stakeholders and society-wide mobilization to support national response plans. However, prolonged suspension of critical economic activity; continued emergency measures, in some cases associated human rights violations; delayed electoral processes and political transitions; as well as inequalities in access to food and essential services disproportionately affecting the low and other vulnerable groups, including women and girls as well as children caught up in conflict; could merge, in some contexts, to spark unrest, (re)ignite wars or upset fragile peace processes. Hence, the political risks associated with the pandemic require close monitoring and management by national and regional actors. The virus could strike hardest in countries with ongoing conflicts or fragile political transitions. As the pandemic unfolds, we are likely to witness a shift in dynamics in several disputes and a possible deterioration in UN relationships with parties in conflict and communities. Despite increased peacebuilding efforts in recent decades, violence and war, exacerbated by terrorism and the spread of violent extremism, transnational organized crime, and weak institutions, continue to pose a challenge in some areas and will inevitably complicate efforts to tackle the virus.

Similarly gaps in state authority, and disregard for arms embargoes, are still present in some parts of the continent. Criminal groups have become more active in finding new routes and methods to traffic drugs and illicit goods and prey on people's vulnerabilities caused by the loss of income. On 23rd March, the United Nations SecretaryGeneral called for a global ceasefire to fight the COVID-19 pandemic. Echoing the continent's "Silencing the Guns" initiative, the Chairperson of the African Union Commission, Moussa Faki Mahamat, also called for a ceasefire. The Secretary-General also appealed for an end to the escalation of violence targeted at women and girls, including domestic violence, as the pandemic spreads. These efforts have yielded some initial positive responses, with 17 Member States across the continent having endorsed the appeal. In Cameroon, South Sudan, and Sudan, armed groups announced temporary unilateral ceasefires.

Nevertheless, these responses remain fragile and reversible. In Libya, a humanitarian truce's announcement has proved tenuous, as both parties to the conflict continue their military operations on the ground. Despite one of the major armed separatist groups having responded positively to the Secretary General's call, violence has also continued in Cameroon. In Somalia, Al-Shabaab has intensified attacks. In the Central African Republic, calls for a cease-fire have not been thoroughly followed, with continuing clashes resulting in dozens killed.

Adapting Democratic Participation To Covid-19

In 2020, at least 22 African countries are scheduled to hold elections, including nine for the president's position. Several states have already held elections since the WHO declared the pandemic. Some countries appear set to proceed with elections as planned or are deliberating their feasibility, while others have decided to postpone polls. Delays might be particularly sensitive in countries with highly polarized political landscapes or countries without constitutional provisions for interim governance. In Somalia, the elections to be held by the end of the year mark an important political milestone. In such settings, inclusive and sustained political dialogue can be vital to mitigating tensions around elections. In countries opting to proceed with elections, governments will need to balance conducting credible elections and ensuring COVID-19 preventive measures' effectiveness. Broad stakeholder consultations are essential in this regard, including with national electoral authorities and public health officials.

Additionally, women candidates, who often have fewer resources and time to spend on a campaign, maybe disproportionately affected by postponed elections or elections taking place under local conditions. Decisions on holding or postponing elections need to be inclusive and should ensure women's participation. UN good offices and election-related technical support remain available to the Member States.

CHAPTER 8
COVID-19: MYSTERIES AND CONSPIRACIES

The issue of conspiracy theories having been a new thing as this have been a long debate and human presumptuous arrival that contradicts what everyone believes is the correct turn-out of an event or the official scheduling of an event which have happened or which is in motion and which is disagreed upon in some quarters that the alleged original result was altered as a aim taking to satisfy some selfish desires of individuals, society or the government.

Tagging along a worldwide health crisis and outbreaks which have shook the world and put a halt on major backbone of the world, it is not quite surprising that they have also stirred up conspiracies as to sudden emergence of such epidemic which sweeps a major proportion of the world population and literally make the world desolate and seeming irreparable. Such epidemic with such importance is the Black Death which killed approximately 500 million people of the world. Even if it had occurred in periods were there was no media coverage or which information dissemination wasn't as developed and efficient like we have in our fingertips these days, nevertheless it has also spurn up old dust and have generated considerable conspiracy theories as people have said it is literally impossible to wipe out that amount of people from the face of the earth at a go, it had to be the work of psychopaths. Other suggested that the figures were over recorded as in that time they were known efficient proper system for the accurate processing of data and facts. Another pandemic which have garnered considerable conspiracy theory over the years is the 20th Century spread of the Spanish Flu which occurred just after the First World War which is on record as the one of the most fatal wars ever fought on the face of the earth. The Spanish Flu pandemic also was reported to have killed millions of people and rendered many jobless and homeless. It was on record that this pandemic was one of the fatal health crisis the world have ever recorded and even with this there are still conspiracy theories flying around today that it was planned before hand as a weapon of war to take out the weak before it all got of control and almost all the population of the world was infected of it.

With the emergence of the Coronavirus pandemic which started late 2019 and which have crippled major sectors of governance and have rendered human's technological and social advancement helpless has it has defied all known form of human medicinal intervention. With the urgency and immediacy in which the coronavirus came up, it has understandably attracted diverse conspiracy theories as many people world over are bringing up their drawn-up analysis daily as to the severity of the virus and the factors surrounding where it emanated from and how it is spreading.

Conspiracy has been built on the idea that the coronavirus is not new, a suspicion that has manifested transversely across countries. Origin-based theories defend the artificial nature of the virus, which spread either accidentally or intentionally. The accident-centered thread blames without evidence; the virus spread on the actors involved' carelessness, who conducted convert activities (e.g., a bioweapon program went wrong). The exploitation of resources and consumers are also pillowed as some suggest a relation of causality between the epidemic and intensive breeding.

Multiple Russian sources of deformation subsequently echoed in other countries, emphasizing the pandemic's bacteriological war intent with assumptions that it originated in the United States of America or China. Accordingly, the virus was created in a lab. It was released voluntarily to achieve geopolitically (e.g., a made-up story circulated in Italy that an American veteran was paid to spread the virus to Europe) or economic gains (e.g., A French research center was accused of creating the virus in 2004 to sell its patented vaccine). The disease was initially reported to WHO on December 31st, 2019. On January 30th, 2020, WHO declared the COVID-19 outbreak a global health emergency, and on March 11th, 2020, it was said a global pandemic by WHO. In late March and early April, President Trump of the United States of America repeatedly proclaimed that hydroxychloroquine could prevent or treat COVID-19. Within a few days, the number of prescriptions for the drug increased even though there was no substantial evidence of its efficacy in treating the viral disease.

Trends of conspiracy theories vs. facts:

Since the advent of the coronavirus pandemic, different type and forms of conspiracy theory have been developed by several individuals and groups. One of the most popular and most concerning theory with the coronavirus theory is the issue of the 5G technology of which its creation and deployment coincidentally also fell with the building up of the coronavirus pandemic.

The emergence of the 5G technology which is also known as the 5th generation technology has been an issue of concern among many people which in fact has led to the creation of several groups which are against its creation. Conspiracy theories have built up even from anti-government agency and groups which had led to riot, unrest and also the dismantling of 5G towers and also telecom masts across major cities of the world. There has also been fire been set up to destroy set up masts as well as the 5G by conspiracy theories do spread the Covid-19 through waves which is produced by this mast. To make matters worse, the conspiracy theory about 5G technology spreading the coronavirus is spreading like wild fires in the social media and networks and this is even enabled by top class citizens, groups, celebrities and even the government which have even created more fear in the mind of citizens due to its wild spread. Some conspiracy theory which have emerged pertaining the 5G technology been one of the cause of the spread of the coronavirus is that Wuhan, China which is the index city of which the pandemic ensued from got plagued with that huge amount of COVID-19 cases due to the large number of 5G telecommunication masts and towers which were present in the city.

This of course is not true due to the fact that prior to the advent of the novel coronavirus pandemic, there was nothing of such as the deployment of 5G masts in the city of Wuhan. Another of such theories which have been making the rounds in recent months is what theorists claim as a wave transmission in which there were claims that the waves which are emitted by the 5G masts and telecommunication masts do weaken the human immune system which further makes the virus further spread to be dangerous. This of course is nothing but far from the truth as the waves which is transmitted by the 5G infrastructure according to studies is said to be a non-ionizing radiation which of course doesn't cause any harm to human's health.

The study further claims that the waves which 5G infrastructure produces is somehow similar to electromagnetic rays of sunlight which also of fact doesn't cause any major adverse effect to the health of individuals. Furthermore, the World Health Organization (WHO) which is the parent body responsible with any form of health relatable cases has debunked such claims which is been circulated by conspiracy theorists claiming 5G waves damages the health as they have insisted that the 5G networks does not spread COVID-19 and that also the radio waves on the network does not also spread the virus or even weaken the human immune system.

Another conspiracy theory that is been peddled around is concerning the coronavirus been a virus that was bioengineered to achieve the selfish reason of its creators. Some government officials and politicians have been making suggestions that the novel coronavirus or the COVID 19 as it is popularly called is actually a developed bio weapon which was developed and created in a scientific lab. This has come up between the United States and the People Republic of China both accusing one another of the creator and the manufacturer of the coronavirus disease. Some important politicians in the United State as since the advent of the coronavirus been coming online and publishing articles on the social media accusing China of manufacturing and creating the coronavirus as a bio weapon in order to achieve the claim of the Chinese communist party in making China cripple the world economy and place the socialist nation as the supreme leader of the world. As if that is not enough claim without evidence, these politicians and groups have also called out China of been the culprit of the creation of the virus when the strain of the virus allegedly got leaked from a bio lab in Wuhan which is the virus epi-center.

These claims were also been circulated in the Chinese camp as well as some Chinese groups also have made suggestion that the virus was created in the US and through covert operation of the CIA, the virus was leaked in China as an aim to annihilate the country's growing competition with the United States. This claim is unfounded and baseless as well as the United States till date have been the worst hit nation of the novel coronavirus pandemic of which so many casualties have been recorded. There has therefore been a lack of evidence which supports both countries' claim of creating the virus and also there have been a valid scientific evidence which is in existence debunking the conspiracy theories been peddled around by these two nations.

Furthermore, another conspiracy theory that is making the rounds is about the theory of which is been spread around as regards this is that major government agencies which are secretive deep states devised the coronavirus as a means to regulate the world population as a way to control the flow of money as that those who are in control of money are in control of the world and its infrastructure. It is believed by this theorist that the golden individuals who make up of less than 1% of the world population connived with the government in creating a viable tool of controlling the world population while protecting the lives of themselves and that of their family members. Also, a theory with similarity with this one is that big pharmaceutical companies of the world have since started the creation of a new form of vaccine which makes use of nano technology in which is embedded microchips. This is believed when use will control the activity of the world population and the creators will gain full control of the world's activity. This of course as well as many vile conspiracy theories been spread around is nothing but an unfounded piece of disinformation which in any way is not true. The coronavirus disease or calling it via its code name, COVID-19 is a type of virus which emerged from a family of virus that traces its origination from animals which are zootopic and this family of viruses include the SARS and MERS which is a well-known type of virus of which no known vaccine had been developed as a cure for this. Hence, the spreading of such theory of the coronavirus pandemic has a measure of population control is unfounded and also baseless in all quarters. In fact, while making comparisons between the coronavirus with the likes of SARS; it was projected by experts as been less deadly when put side by side with SARS. According to these reports, the coronavirus mortality rate was put at 2.3% with regards to the number of infection and casualties which results from it, while SARS was reported to be put at 9.6% which is of no doubt greater than the mortality rate of the coronavirus disease. Hence the theory of the coronavirus disease been a weapon of population control is proved wrong as a mere speculation which is based on unsupported facts.

Political manipulation or how to use secret agenda:
conspiracy theories advocate private plots that the powerful elites hide from the public's eye to manipulate the people politically. Many forms

of conspiracies have been ongoing in several countries owing to how the government has used the COVID-19 as a tool for getting funds from other nations. Thus there have been trends of speculations that the number of confirmed cases has been inflated.

In Nigeria, for instance, there are reports that some patients who visited the hospital gave information about how a mere malaria case was recorded as a COVID-19 case. In Nigeria, the citizens are still puzzled about how the Nigeria Centre for Disease Control (NCDC) treats the COVID-19 patients since WHO has canceled hydroxychloroquine. Many Nigerians still doubt the NCDC testing capacity. In a viral video released via social media, a lady was seen dancing continuously to the chorus "Do you know somebody who knows somebody, who has corona," Which calls the coronavirus, especially in Nigeria, a hoax.

The majority of Nigerians are apoplectic, noting that even at such a high number of COVID-19 cases, none of them have ever seen a victim of the disease. The only ones they have seen in a video are just a group of NCDC officials engaging in mortal combat with their accused victims. Also, there have been claims in Nigeria at the beginning of the lockdown due to the pandemic that political activities were still holding while schools, markets, worship centers were closed. In recent times, in Kaduna, Nigeria, all the shops at Kaduna Central Market have been completed to reduce the large gathering of people. Sadly, all the shop owners resorted to displaying their products on the street, outside the primary market, consequently leading to congestion of people, thereby making the initial intent for the market closure futile. A further step in the narrative conspiracy proposes the reluctance of the government to communicate the real situation. Accordingly, the goal is to push an undemocratic and unethical agenda that would cause public upheavals if known.

Population cleansing is a general theory that emerged in different terms: examples of conspiracy theories in this class include claims that China created the virus to solve the overpopulation problem. In Europe, the virus was to eliminate the elderly. In Nigeria, the conspiracy theory is that the virus has come to eradicate the country's corrupt political leaders. It is also feared that the pandemic will be used as an excuse to imposed meddles mass vaccination, whose real purpose is to implement an Orwellian mechanism of social control. Other conspiracy theories suggest that the lockdown is an excuse to force people into their homes while authoritarian measures are being implemented. A common goal is to show the collusion of political and economic powers for evil intent.

Evergreen Conspiracies Step into the shoes of COVID-19: besides the extensively explored deep state allegations, other conspiracy theories that do not entirely fit the previous narratives include:

1) The prophetic origin of SARS-CoV-2 was foreseen by Nostradamus, Bill gates, or The Simpsons.

2) A revival of anti-Semitism accusing Jewish communities of speeding the virus for the purpose of poisoning the gentiles and sacrificing them as part of religious rituals.

3) Finally, the 5G conspiracy has also become a narrative of its own primed in Europe and beyond. Popular claims are that SARS-CoV-2 is transmitted through 5G antennas and that the 5G technology has a negative health impact and thus makes individuals vulnerable to the virus.

Cure and medical treatment conspiracy theories: a number of conspiracy theories confuse the long-standing existence of COVID-19, therefore claiming that the cure already existed and in line with the theory of power, the elite had refused to share it with the whole population. To illustrate this, in France, some groups of Facebook users met the news of the speedy recovery of Prince Charles despite his old age with suspicion. In Nigeria, there have been many conspiracies about the existence of the disease owing that many of the mortality cases occur in the elderly age and there has been a trend that people in the age died of a merely terminal disease that is co-infection rather than due to the virus. According to research which was carried out by the Solidarity Trials International Steering committee which was later accepted and approved by the World Health Organization; WHO showed that the drug hydroxychloroquine and some anti-viral drugs Like lopinavir/ritonavir produce little or no reduction in the mortality of hospitalized COVID-19 patients when compared to standard of care, WHO accepted their recommendation and discontinued the treatment of COVID-19 patients with hydroxychloroquine and lopinavir/ritonavir. In a recent video released by Dr. Stella Immanuel, she made an unsubstantial claim that hydroxychloroquine is a cure for COVID-19, the disease caused by

SARS-CoV-2. She also claimed that she had cured about 350 coronavirus patients noting that a mixture of hydroxychloroquine, azithromycin, and zinc sulfate is a permanent cure for their virus. She also added that neither faces masks nor lockdown is necessary to fight the pandemic. She accused other doctors, health practitioners, and political heads of state of concealing the truth from the people. Her video was also retweeted by Trump to show his support. The video was deleted by all social media platforms and termed to be violating COVID-19 rules and misleading. Remember that Trump had also frozen US government funding to WHO due to conspiracy on how it handles COVID-19 pandemic. Also, recall that Madagascar purported a homemade herbal cure for coronavirus, which the president, Andry Rajoelina, applauded and also added that he was paid millions of dollars by WHO to discontinue the production of the drug, but as of 9th August, the number of confirmed COVID-19 patients has reached to 13,086 with about 2,122 active cases and 148 deaths. One will question if the herbal drug does not work again?

CHAPTER 9
THE GREAT ECONOMIC AND FINANCIAL RESET

IMPACT ON GLOBAL BUSINESS:

The coronavirus pandemic which have been around for a while have cause unprecedented damage to the workings and safe functioning of major parts of all sectors of the economy. It has led to untold halt in the production of goods, agricultural produce and has also threatened the mining, aviation and all other manufacturing industries. So many employers of labours have been affected as well as farmers which have led to more loss of jobs done by them. With the temporary closure of business which had led to the slowing down of normal economy process of the global world and has proved worse for the global economy, most nations of the world are been affected and this also is pulling down the economy globally. One of the countries which were affected early on by the impact of the viral disease is China which is the 2nd largest economy in the world behind the United States. China which is the epicentre of the coronavirus disease had prompted the government of the socialist nation to call for a lockdown and closure of businesses and industries. This has led to the closure of manufacturing companies and major technological industries and has ultimately led to the reduction in activities and production of these companies and has crippled the economy of the country. Also, the United States which is world's largest company and is the widely hit of the disease has also suffered shock on its economy as different manufacturing company and industries have been forced to shut down temporarily. Generally, with the uncertainty of which the ravaging COVID-19 poses, there is an expectation for the volatility and inconsistencies of the global market of which no global growth or development in the economy is not expected to occur this year. To obtain a growth in the global market and further ensure the development of the world economy, the governments, policy makers and stakeholders are been encouraged to review policies and guidelines provided in an aim to mitigate the ravaging effect of the virus on the economy.

It has been a year and some months since the outbreak of the deadly coronavirus disease and the global economy of the world has been greatly affected by the adverse effect of the coronavirus disease as even with the rebound that is been seen across some economies globally is been poised to be uneven and even some economies even still at their worst level in history. In fact, global growth of economy is said to be 5.6% which considerably due to the contribution of the world's largest economies i.e. USA and China. But this recovery is still considered to be pretty little as compared to what the economies have suffered in the previous year that was riddled with the pandemic. Let us take a look at the impacts which the different sectors of the global economy as felt due to the coronavirus disease.

Let us take the agricultural sector as an example, the advent of the coronavirus pandemic which have hit the world in a very awkward way, the agricultural sector have been badly hit as the level of production and the amount of produce from this sector have gradually reduced which is a thing that have been a major concern to the major shareholders in government.

According to the Australian Bureau of Resource Economics and Sciences, the largest threat to agricultural firms comes from declining global incomes, which will likely drive prices down. Declining export demand for produce has increased local supply, placing downward price pressure for some goods. For example, seafood prices have declined due to reduced demand from export markets and the food-service sector. However, prices for other items, such as beef, are anticipated to rise as farmers take the opportunity to rebuild their herds, reducing supply.

Falling global retail sales are expected to negatively affect demand for cotton and wool as apparel companies reduce production. This trend is anticipated to reduce prices and revenue generated by Australian cotton and wool growers. (Source: Ibbs industry review)

In other sub sectors of the agricultural sector which have been diversely affected by the coronavirus pandemic is the wood and pulp industry. According to reports, some countries' wood and logging industries have experienced considerable setbacks due to the coronavirus pandemic has some sawmills and wood processing factories have undergone closedown and closures. Additionally, the closure of upstream pulp and wood chip manufacturers has forced some industry operators to suspend operations despite steady demand for products like toilet paper and paper towels which are essentials for human use.

Concerns about the potential transmission of the coronavirus among animals will require further monitoring. Previous outbreaks, such as the swine flu and bird flu, have shown the ability to spread among humans and animals. At this time, all reports indicate than transmission from animals to humans is not possible. Pork production has dropped in China due to both coronavirus and African swine fever outbreaks, driving up global producer prices. As one of the most prevalent producers of pork, the global market is directly affected by this. Due to the closure of many inner-European borders, farmers are lacking Eastern European harvest helpers for asparagus harvesting and spring sowing of other vegetables. This could lead to a shortage of domestic fruit and vegetable supply. Milk production is massively affected by the coronavirus, leading to falling milk prices. Although the demand for dairy products from supermarkets is rising sharply, the demand from large consumers like restaurants or hotels has declined significantly. The dairies are already calling for a reduction in milk production.

Also another important area of agricultural sector which have been adversely affected by the coronavirus pandemic outbreak is the fishing section which unfortunately have suffered major setbacks due to the ravaging effect of the coronavirus pandemic. The outbreak has caused a severe demand shock for most fish farmers, as a result of plunging demand from export markets and domestic restaurants. Since the government has issued lockdown, most farmers haven't been able to make distribution of their harvest fishes and other marine animals and due to the shortage of demand, there have been shortages which have led to untold hardship to fishing business.

In general, the impacts of the coronavirus pandemic on the agricultural sector of the economy is a thing of fright and have done worse than good to it. Several efforts and short-term policies have since been devised by the government and also by private investors in order to minimize the consequences of the impact of the coronavirus pandemic on the agricultural business.

Another sector which the Covid-19 is the transportation sector, Without much doubt, there has been a great ravaging effect of the coronavirus pandemic on the transportation sector of the economy, this is the due to the fact that government of all nations world over have issued compulsory lockdown to all their citizens which is a measure taken to limit the spread of the coronavirus in their respective country or states. Due to this unfortunate incidence but necessary safety precautionary foresight, transportation in and out of city states and even international and intercontinental travels have been suspended and all form of travels have been placed on ban until there is limited or no rate of contraction is been recorded globally. All subsectors of the transportation industry have had their awkward share of the unfortunate calamity that has since befall all nation of the world. Sectors of transportation like aviation, marine, rail and road transportation have been affected. Most major investors and shareholders have been lamenting their losses ever since the breakout of the pandemic which have wrought havoc to all sectors of the world economy and sub-economy.

Taking a look at the aviation sector for example which inarguably have been the hardest hit of the coronavirus pandemic which have posed serious and tough challenges on the workability and proper functioning of airlines, airports and also the ecosystem and habitat. The pandemic is currently wreaking havoc on the global aviation industry as major investments and top airlines in the world with likes of American Airlines and Virgin Atlantic have been laying off their staff most especially non-essential workers with the aim of managing the massive negative impact in which the pandemic have brought on the sector. They have also begun to deploy most of their passenger aircraft to carry on cargo goods like medical supplies and also perishable products in a aim to help the government to expedite the provision of social welfare and packages to the people and relieving the effect caused by the coronavirus pandemic. Also, major airliners and airbus owners around the world have since grounded most of their commercial passenger flight which include brands such as British Airways which have grounded all their flights at their base at the Airport. The aviation transportation industry have been hit with massive huge uncertainty following the outbreak of the coronavirus pandemic in almost all parts of the world which have been a thing of concern to major stakeholders in this industry and also giving investors new insights on how to further make significant technological advancement on the industry in order to further prevent the losses experienced in the future.

Reduced passenger traffic for example in the aviation industry is forcing stakeholders and major players in the industry to set aside more funds for the development of high mobile drones and also programmed vehicles which help to tackle such challenges in the future and also in a way to serve the whole ecosystem. The coronavirus pandemic have also offered much threat to job security of workers working within the aviation industry as study has shown that an estimate of one in five jobs in areas affected by the coronavirus is at risk which is a thing of major concern.

Also, looking at other sub-sectors of the transportation sector of the economy like the road and the rail sector which also have incurred significant losses due to the impact caused by the coronavirus pandemic which have wrought havoc in major sectors of the world economy with transportation as no exception. According to studies, it have been confirmed that four of 10 people polled have said that they won't make use of public transportation which is mainly buses, trains and other form of transits until they feel they are safe. This is due to the fact that people are becoming well concerned about social distancing and the use of face masks as the measures brought up by the government ever since the partial relaxing of the lockdown ruled earlier put forward to curtail the spread of the coronavirus pandemic among people. Many people still feel uneasy in boarding public transits as they feel the probability of contracting the viral infection is high as not everyone will follow government and health organizations directive of the maintenance of the stipulated social distancing rules.

The Entertainment industry as well which is a major and key generation of wealth and revenue for the economy was adversely affected by the coronavirus pandemic. The entertainment industry and the entire universe around it have come to a standstill. Never in history had the entertainment industry witnessed such desolation that the COVID-19 pandemic has made it go through.

Across the showbiz industry be which consists of the American movie and Indian movie industry, even if we take a conservative estimate the loss will be in billions of dollars. The unfortunate emergence of the coronavirus pandemic across the world have put fear in the heart of many as many predicts it is a dark era of the theatre and showbiz industry and it will take years for this respected industry to recover. The world crisis is a crippling blow for the industry and one can't be certain about the time it will take to recover and function in full swing. It is a huge blow to everyone who have over the years been impacted by the movie industry hovering from the filmmakers, directors, actors, show-runners and most importantly the viewers who have over time been the major consumers of the goodies brought forward by the entertainment industry and show-biz world in general. As the world is still undergoing and in the midst of a pandemic in which no one saw coming, this have put a major halt on production and release of blockbuster movies and theatrical performance earlier slated to be released over the course of the year and have since suffered a major backdrop and setback due to the ravaging effect of the coronavirus pandemic. Because theatrical releases are not possible, major movies will either have their release dates delayed or go directly to streaming services. In fact, it is already happening. This will have major ramifications for movie theatres, marketing agencies and studios.

Re-budgeting for marketing, loss of ticket sales, concessions, the fallout of collaborations and so on will occur. Although the shutdown have only lasted for a little time of about two months but in that short time frame, the pandemic has brought the film, television and even the music business to their dilemma. The impact of the pandemic on the showbiz business have been one of the greatest hit on the industry in recent times aside such catastrophe wrecking moment like the 9/11 and the great depression. According to study reported, it have been reported that the film and television industry employs and have employment deals with approximately close to 900,000 people which are direct staffs or contract workers. With the emergence of the pandemic which have wrought wreckage, the figures of those that have lost and will lose their source of livelihood is still unknown but it has been estimated that close to 200,000 of this employees are to be laid off. These figures consist majorly of non-essential or theatre add-on staffs like ushers or other back up staffs all of whom most of them have been laid off and relieved off their source of livelihood. Also another large proportion which is about 32% of these employees of the entertainment and TV industry which consists of actors, directors, producers, script writers and other production workers which have been left with nothing to do due to the lockdown orders by the government as a measure of curtailing the spread of the coronavirus pandemic.

Most of the workers working in the entertainment industry have been exposed and the edge of the standard of living these workers were living before the outbreak has come to light. Most of the workers who work during and tag along the physical production of movies aren't actually full time workers as they are majorly freelance workers who are working in between jobs in order to make ends meet and have a source of sustaining livelihood and since the emergence of the pandemic, some of them have been forced to submit applications to unemployment agencies as they have been forced out of jobs. Although some companies and establishments such as Netflix and Viacom and also some movie unions have collaborated to start funding as a way of providing support to individuals who have been laid off or have lost jobs due to the shutdown. This have helped the laid off workers to have hope although they are worried that it wouldn't be enough to run to summer or the load will be too much on the support agencies if the lockdown should stretch up till the summer.

Furthermore, the impact of the coronavirus pandemic is also been felt on business and little establishment which are solely dependent on the theatre and TV industry. The little businesses that are been affected ranges from floral businesses to hair stylists and also food catering services who also have considerable impact on the entertainment industry as to lunch provision for hungry casts and crews. It is still uncertain when movie production will resume and in which most theatres will open for teeming viewers to come in and watch what they love to see well. Most people who have either been laid off or which in one way or another been offered jobless due to the coronavirus pandemic will most possibly come back to the business which is unrecognizable to them. Even when the cameras eventually begin to roll out, there are expectations that the audiences and theatre viewers will have to be subjective to the periodic wearing of masks and the practice of the social distancing guideline. Also, performers and crew members will be regularly subjected to temperature checking and also routine and periodic testing of the viral infection. This also will bore challenge on the filmmakers and major stakeholders in the theatre and TV industry due to logical reasons which will add more production costs and cause budgets allocated to films to skyrocket and also will add more days to the time taken in shooting a film.

It is clear that all major stakeholders in the theatre industry which include studios and trade union workers are working around the clock and are trying the best they can to make sure people around the theatre and entertainment industry get back to work sooner. But a theory abounds that the minimal number people on set will likely reduce the rate of the spread of the coronavirus which means fewer jobs will be available around for people to take. With that the production company might want to offer lower pay with the assurance that people will want to take the rare opportunity as work is not in abundance in the first place.

CHAPTER 10
VACCINE DEVELOPED BY DIFFERENT PLAYERS

Ever since the declaration of the outbreak of the coronavirus disease as a global pandemic by the World Health Organization earlier this year, scientists globally have begun to work on devising potential treatments and also formulate vaccines and anti-viral pills which will help to annihilate the spread and severity of the coronavirus. Several companies and government funded institutions have since started to find a way to devise a cure that helps the immune system in the fight against COVID-19, some of these vaccines been worked upon were already in use against previously discovered life-threatening illnesses and diseases. Other efforts are been made to develop a vaccine or functioning drug that can be used as a preventive measure against the coronavirus disease.

Some clinical testing have been in full flow ever since and there have been considerable improvement as with the improvement of drugs which have been proven to have offered resistance against well-known disease. Some of the vaccine and drugs been worked upon and have also received emergency authorization use by the government agencies who are burdened with the safety and proper workings of vaccine are the chloroquine and hydroxychloroquine which have made considerable effort in previous years with the cure of the malaria disease and also a known anti-viral vaccine which is the remdesivir. Several biotech and pharmaceutical companies have been said to have recorded considerable improvement with the development of vaccine to tackle the coronavirus pandemic.

A small firm which are specialized in formulating biotechnology drugs have said they have developed an antibody drug that have been proven to be effective in blocking genomes and virus that results in COVID 19 at an early stage and also help in preventing infection. These drugs moreover are still been tested in trials to see if they are really effective against the coronavirus and forming a long-term cure of the deadly infection. With these vaccines still undergoing clinical trials to verify its safety for use and also cut out the side effects which may be generated with its use, it means it can still take months before viable treatments and cure are available to work against the coronavirus disease. But even with that, there seems to be a ray of light in the sky as to the successful management of the coronavirus disease and there exists other tools or means which can help reduce the damage done by the coronavirus disease.

Bringing forth a new vaccine to the public do involve that so many steps are carried out which includes the development of the vaccine itself, clinical trials carried out, the authorization and the approval of the vaccine developed and tried over series of phases, the manufacturing of these vaccines in large numbers and finally the effective distribution of these vaccines to people. Since the outbreak of the coronavirus pandemic, so many stakeholders which includes both public and private stakeholders have been working around the clock to ensure the quick roll-out of the vaccines and also to ensure that all steps is taken to ensure the safe usage and the functionality of the vaccine without creating another scare through side effects.

Drug developments have been regarded as pipelines as the process is both tasking and also chows time and resources. This is due to the fact that the process of formulation of viable vaccine needed to tackle a disease either viral, bacterial and the likes is arduous. It borders on the movement of compounds from early laboratory stages down to clinical and animal testing before been inoculated in humans as a form of clinical testing. This is why drugs been used in curtailing the coronavirus disease presently are vaccine drugs that are known to have existed previously. Many of the drugs been devised and developed to use in tackling the coronavirus are drugs known to be anti-viral as it would target the genetic sequence of the virus in people known to have been infected with the virus.

The development of vaccines initially starts out from the laboratory which includes studying the virus and the causative agents that causes the virus. The virus which causes the Covid-19 virus is a virus that is related to other coronaviruses variants that leads to severe acute respiratory syndrome codenamed SARS as well as the Middle East respiratory syndrome codenamed MERS. The need for the research is to quickly compare the results of the study obtained with the results of past researches on viruses that are similar to the variant of the SARS-COV2 as this will help to accelerate the development of the vaccines.

After the study and the initial development of the vaccine prototype have been carried out, the next thing to come up is the carrying out of clinical trials of which the vaccine developed is subjected to scrutinized testing over three phases so as to make sure the vaccine is safe to use as well as effective. These phases are usually carried out consecutively of which it takes place one phase at a time instead of combining the three phases together but with the wide spread of the Covid-19 pandemic, it has prompted the quick trial to be carried out on the vaccines of which the three phases overlapped so as to ensure the quick distribution of the vaccine to achieve control over the pandemic. The clinical trials were carried out with the help of so many volunteers so as to control the widespread of the pandemic of which the results from the trials have shown the effectiveness of the vaccines. These trials have proven to be a very great step towards the rollout of the vaccines by different players and nations in controlling the spread of the virus.

The development of the vaccines also involved the manufacturing as well as the distribution in large doses of the vaccines developed so as to control the spread of the coronavirus disease. The United States for example have invested substantial number of resources towards the manufacturing of the vaccines even at the third phase of the clinical trials carried out so as to ensure the quick distribution of the vaccines. Looking away from the manufacturing and the distribution of the vaccines used to mitigate the effect of the Covid-19 disease, there exists monitoring systems also put in place by the different stakeholders of which ensures the tracking of the vaccines to ensure the safety of the administering of these vaccines. This monitoring is needed so as to handle any side-effects or complain that may arise from people after vaccination.

A lot of focus has been on the developments of new treatments for the treating of the coronavirus and as well as the improvements in the general pharmaceutical and medicinal developments. Also there has been focus on the development and advancement in the usage of trado-medicinal drugs and vaccines in the treatment of the Coronavirus disease which have been a source of global challenge to the world at large. Efforts have been made in this aspect as some nations have already allegedly developed a viable cure that can be used as a cure for the coronavirus disease. A notable one is the Covid organics vaccine allegedly reported to be an alternative cure aside well-known western medicine for the prevention and curing of the viral infection. This drug was reported to have been created from wild plants and also herbs and allegedly issue a sort of resistance to the coronavirus in the immune system.

There hasn't been a stipulated timeframe as to when vaccines will be ready for use and widely regarded as a treatment of the coronavirus infection. This is due to the fact that even after laboratory testing, drugs still have to go through series of trials and phases before it can be used as a widespread treatment for people. Also, it also proves difficult to speed up the development of drugs up as scientists need to wait long enough to see about the safety of drugs and the impact such drugs can make to human life. Also there have been well improved testing which have been reported in a way to reduce the mortality of the coronavirus by slowing down the spread of the viral infection.

EFFORTS PUT IN PLACE BY COUNTRIES
- **China**

Countries such as China and Russia have also been coming up with their own vaccine of which some haven't been out there due to the pending approving from the World Health Organization. WHO however has authorized the first rollout of the COVID-19 vaccines which is been used for emergency while some are still being listed. This listing according to researchers and experts has been seen to boost the global confidence in the vaccines developed for the cure against coronavirus and even based on the fact that it is coming from China which is the origination of the deadly virus in the first instance.

The first of the vaccines to listed made in China by the State-owned factory is the Sinopharm of which speculations are going on that its name is the CoronaVac. These vaccines reportedly are tested on inactivated viruses and therefore are not widely made used of around the globe especially among Western nations. Both Sinopharm as well as Sinovac's rolled out vaccines do account for the bulk of shots that is made given by China of which about 250 million have benefited from the vaccine rollout and more than 45 countries also have already approved for their use although the WHO are still reviewing the data of its usage as well as its effectiveness.

There also have been the development of another vaccine called Coronovac by China of which was produced and developed by a pharmaceutical company that is based in Beijing and based on the inactivated form of the SARS-CoV2 virus. All of these vaccines as listed developed above are known to require two doses instead of the single dose that some devised human adenovirus gives out.

The administration of these vaccines as developed by China have been impressive according to the data produced by the National Health Commission of which about 120 million doses of the vaccines have been administered and that the country is still aiming to vaccinate

40% of the country's population of 1.4 billion just at the beginning of August 2021. The country also is tending to prioritize giving out the vaccines to keyworkers of the economy of whose age falls between 18 and 59 before starting the distribution of vaccines to more vulnerable members of the population of who are aged 60 or above.

Outside of the republic of China, China's vaccines which included the first vaccines engineered by Sinopharm has received the most approvals for emergency usage among countries such as Bahrain, Guyana, Serbia and the UAE. Among European nations, Hungary was the first country in Europe to approve of the use of the Chinese vaccine. Aside the Sinopharm, several countries have also approved the use of the CoronaVac jab for emergency usage. Countries such as Brazil who have been badly hit by the coronavirus wave have issued the emergency use of the CoronaVac vaccine as well as Chile where the vaccines where trialed as well. Other countries who have also authorized the use of the CoronaVac from China includes Indonesia, Laos, Mexico as well as Turkey.

Although some of the vaccines that are being produced by China are being accessed by different nations, especially smaller ones but the WHO hasn't fully approved it which leaves a shortfall in the accessing of China made vaccines by smaller countries. But in recent times, this is starting to get tackled through the COVAX which is an initiative put in place by international partnerships as well as WHO to ensure that the COVID-19 vaccines are distributed well among nations.

- **Russia**

There also have been the development of vaccines by Russia. In fact, the vaccine developed by Russia which was named Sputnik have garnered different reactions as well as opinions from the world since it was authorized for usage by the Russian government. This vaccine was in fact released and authorized by the Russian government even before the publication of early-stage trial results of the effectiveness of the vaccine.

However, evidences have been arising from Russia as well as other countries which are suggesting the effectiveness of the Sputnik vaccine although doubts still arise of the side effects which this vaccine may have on the user. So many western countries including the United States were initially dismissive of the effectiveness of this vaccine but with the data that have been coming from trials done on Phase III of the vaccine, there have been the evidence that the vaccine is effective which has sparked up interests from so many people abroad. There have been different claims and order for the Sputnik V vaccine according to official sources like the RDIF of which the Kremlin has suggested that it cannot handle all order which has been coming for these vaccines considering the production capacity of the federation on the vaccines. Therefore, the RDIF have disclosed that supply will be made to foreign market of the vaccines from plants that are stationed outside of Russia and not from the products made for the indigent of Russia as the local made vaccines according to the Kremlin isn't even enough yet to handle the buzzing population of the federation.

VACCINES THAT ARE AUTHORIZED AND IN USE

Developments have been massive on the production of vaccines that helps in the curing of the Covid-19 virus and so many vaccines as well as pharmaceutical medicines have been developed and authorized for usage. These vaccines are in variance with their mode of usage, their percentage effectiveness as well as the side effects which they produce after the vaccination process. Let us look at each and everyone of these vaccines individually.

- **MODERNA**

This is RNA vaccine that was developed by Moderna in Massachusetts, United States and was funded by the National Institute of Allergy and Infectious Diseases (NIAID) which is an institute that is part of the US National Institutes of Health. The final trial of this vaccine result confirms that this vaccine is 94% effective against the variant of the COVID19 disease and this data was sent to regulators around the world.

This vaccine needs to be maintained and kept in a very cool environment which makes it to be placed in ultra-cold freezers. It also has the ability of it to be shipped over a longer distance and kept in storage within freezers that are of the standard temperatures and can also be kept and stored for up to 30 days making use of normal refrigeration which makes it easy to distribute as well as store effectively.

There exists the emergency authorized usage of this vaccine in the US around December 18, 2020 which makes it the second vaccine to have received the authorization of the FDA after the Pfizer vaccine. It is also authorized for usage in most European countries as well as other parts of the world. This vaccine is also recommended for usage among age group of around 18 and older. The dosage of this vaccine is 2 shots of which the days between the initial vaccination and the final one is 28 days.

There is a similarity with the working of this vaccine as well as with the Pfizer vaccine in that it works as an mRNA vaccine that sends the instructions on the body's cells making a spike in the protein in the body that will train the immune system to recognize this and makes it easy for the immune system to attack the spike protein the next time when it sees one which is among the one that is attached to the variant of the SARS CoV-2 virus.

Although there exist some side effects with the administration of this vaccine, it still ranks high as one of the most effective vaccine that helps to treat the COVID19 and even research is showing that this vaccine may provide better protection against the new Alpha and Beta variants of the virus.

- **PFIZER/BIONTECH**

The Pfizer vaccine happened to become the first COVID19 vaccine to receive the Emergency Use Authorization (EUA) from the United States FDA. This was done after the company made a report of positive clinical trial data which included that the vaccine was 95% effective against the coronavirus disease. Also, this vaccine also got the Emergency Use Authorization for its usage in the European Union under the name Comirnaty.

This vaccine is recommended for individuals who are 12 or older and also is a drug that is administered in 2 shots as same as the Moderna vaccine. The only difference in the dosage of this vaccine from the Moderna one is that this is 21 days apart from the initial vaccine administering and the final vaccine administering.

This vaccine is mRNA which makes use of a new technology. This vaccine is also in variance with other vaccines that put a weakened or inactivated disease germ into the body, it delivers a tiny piece of genetic code form the SARS CoV-2 virus to host cells in the body. As with the Moderna virus, this vaccine also gives instructions to the cells as well as creation of blueprints which creates the making of copies of spike proteins. These spikes help in the penetration and the infection of the host cells. These proteins also in return stimulate an immune response which helps in the production of antibodies and the development of memory cells that will recognize the spikes and respond when the body is infected with the COVID19 virus.

This vaccine was found out to be more than 95% effective against severe diseases from the Alpha variant and the Beta variant which are mutations of the original strain of virus that was discovered in Wuhan, China. Studies has shown that the vaccine provides strong protection against these variants.

- **JOHNSON & JOHNSON**

The FDA granted the emergency use approval of this vaccine on February 27, 2021 for the prevention against a different type of vaccine which is called the carrier or virus vector. This vaccine unlike the other two that are as listed above is easily available for storage as it can be stored in refrigerator temperature instead of ultra-cold storage. This vaccine requires the use of only a single shot which makes it easier for the distribution and the administering of this vaccine. This vaccine is also being shown according to data available to reduce the spread of the virus by individuals who have used this drug for vaccination.

This vaccine obtained its authorization of usage in the U.S as well as authorization to be made used of in the European Union under the name Janssen. The dosage of this drug is also single shot which is in variance with the dosage of both the Pfizer as well as the Moderna vaccines. Although, there are some researches and extensive studies going on by the producer of this vaccine of launching a second Phase III clinical trial to study the usage of two doses of which the administer date will be in between two months so as to see the best one that provides the better protection against the different variants of the coronavirus disease.

The J&J vaccine is a carrier vaccine that makes a different approach than the mRNA vaccines in that it instructs human cells to make the spiking of protein through the SARS CoV-2. This therefore is a human adenovirus. It works through the creation of a sort of Trojan Horse of which there is the engineering of a shell to carry genetic code on the spike proteins to the cell. This spike and code once in the body doesn't cause sickness but the code only helps to produce a spike protein that will help to train the immune system of the body which creates the antibodies as well as the memory cells to protect against the actual SARS-CoV-2 infection.

The effectiveness of this vaccine has been found to offer protection against the Alpha variant of which data from the FDA shows 64% overall efficacy against the Alpha variant and an overall 82% efficacy against severe disease caused by the Beta Variant. Also there have also been some promises seen against the new Delta variant of which the vaccine has shown a small drop in its potency compared with the effectiveness against the original strain of the virus.

- **AZTRAZENECA**

This is the vaccine that is been distributed in the UK as well as other countries in Europe. This vaccine makes for its competition with other vaccines in that it has lower cost and it is cheaper to make per dose as well as its storage, transportation and distribution can be done using normal refrigeration for at least 6 months. This vaccine is only been distributed in the European Union and not available for use in the US.

Its dosage is two doses between four to 12 weeks apart but which is a carrier vaccine made from a harmless adenovirus. This vaccine is seen to be 75% effective against the Alpha variant of the COVID19 disease and also 85% in people who have never shown symptoms of the Coronavirus.

The development of these different vaccines as well as the efforts which are being made by different stakeholders has helped to greatly reduce the number of cases as well as the rate of hospitalizations to manageable rate for so many countries which have brought about the removal and relaxation of different restrictions put up to curtail the spread of the disease.

This development gives hope that the COVID19 will be defeated and the world will be returned back to normalcy of which people will move about their day-to-day activities.

CHAPTER 11
WORKING FROM HOME AS THE NORMAL

The coronavirus pandemic which has thrown the world into a state of disarray and have brought down so many challenges to literally all the people of the world have been a major challenge to world leaders and government organizations as well due to the fact that this deadly and dangerous pandemic which is ravaging on a daily basis do not respect anyone. It has been a challenge for everyone ranging especially for the government at the centre in which are tasked with the responsibility of formulating policies and measures which can help limit the spread of the coronavirus disease and also down to the lower cadre which are the citizenry who also are faced with the issue of taking heed to the government's directive and guidelines while also providing needed support to one another. The coronavirus which have called for the prompt reaction and policy stipulation by the government which in recent months have called for the needed closure of places of work, schools, offices, markets, airports and public places generally. These have placed a large proportion of people in the compulsory lockdown and unable to move out and conduct their normal business proceedings. The coronavirus pandemic have left people of the world in desperate situation to survive as they are faced with the dangers of the ravaging pandemic and also not able to work in providing for their families. The world is now confronted with reality in the sense of the true essence of human existence and also the vulnerabilities which are posed with the existence of the human species. The true essence of existence is now brought forward to each and every one of us has we have been brought into answering basic life questions which is about our existence, the people and individuals which we cherish and also evaluating what is really important to us.

The Coronavirus disease which for more than a year has been declared by the WHO as a global pandemic has changed a lot of things of how things most especially work is being carried out as working from home is now to be the new normal as to which business can be conducted. For most workers, the transition to working from home has been seen as quite a shock to many workers as there were uncertainties on how productive as well efficient, they can be from working from home.

Since the Covid-19 virus has called for the working from home of different workers due to lockdown measures enacted by the government in order to curtain the effect of the coronavirus, working remotely is now the normal which is a new hybrid way of working and this will of a fact affect the mode of communication, creation and connection of workers. But with the emergence of video conferencing systems and platforms such as Zoom, MS Teams, Google meet and others such as email and messaging apps platforms has made the working from home to make them more productive in fact in some ways, more productive than the normal office work they are well acclimatized with.

But will working from home continue to be the norms of things even in the nearest future, well it seems to be so. According to surveys that has been conducted among workers on how working from home has affected them as well as if they'll like to continue with working from home, most of them cited that they feel comfortable and better working from home of which many has already began the expansion of their home offices as well as designation of workspaces so as to prepare to work from home as long as they could do that. This has led to the falling in prices of office spaces in big cities and metropolis such as London, Dublin, Paris and so many other places and invariably led to the increase in the demand that is made for single-family homes in the suburbs.

Some workers have cited that they pretty much agree to the idea of working from home as there are so many advantages with doing that as they need not need take a commute to work on a daily basis and that they save money more than when they were working in the offices. Also, some disadvantages of working from home was cited by some other group of people such as the inability to know when to stop as there isn't any office hours again which leads to overworking at some point. Another disadvantage cited was the presence of distractions at home as well as having problems with tech. Also, the issue with finding a working and reliable WiFi as well as fatigue incurred with video teleconferencing were also cited as one of the reasons of which they don't prefer remote working to on-site working.

But studies and surveys which have been conducted especially among workers has suggested a more modest shift to the remote working after the pandemic as even a substantial number of on-site workers now adopting a permanent remote working style. But what is the implication of this in the short-term as well as in the long-term based on rents as well as housing costs on an annual basis. Due to the shift in the paradigm to remote working, it has led to the extra costs added to housing as now remote workers that are not earning as much are also been forced to spend big on their rent which has considerably gone up since the pandemic started. And not everyone can just rent an extra work space or even an apartment which they can use as an office while working remotely. But on the upside, the remote workers do not need to spend on commute any longer as they now spend way less on transportation due to working from home. But paying less for transportation is seen to likely make up for the differentials in the rent that is paid for renting and housing as costs of transportation here doesn't make consideration on the amount spent on the maintenance of private vehicles by these workers especially those living in suburban areas.

On the issue of office rents as well as mortgage prices to be paid by office owners, it is pretty a tumbling number especially in big offices as even a long-term abandonment of these offices and this may even change the national landscape of compensation paid as well as the housing cost. The offloading of office space of a fact has become harder for companies that are stuck in leasing on a long-term basis which is creating a major problem of generating profits for them. This also will invariably affect the payment of salaries as well as the foregoing of some bonuses and perks that are offered by the employers to the employees as the employers are now showing not to have interest in raising salaries to reflect the expenses they pay on lower expenses although some companies are now taking another approach which involves announcing the reduction in pay for employees so that they choose to move to lower-cost cities.

Aside from the downside to it, working from home has incredible benefits for companies as well as for their employees due to the pandemic as there have been reported the increase in the amount of productivity that is seen from working from home as well as saving of costs at an optimal level by the employees and working from home can now be seen as a new normal for millions of workers around the world as well as in the foreseeable future.

CONCLUSION

Many conspiracies have evolved due to this novel coronavirus disease, some having some facts that could be true. Amongst all these conspiracies, nevertheless, Coronavirus disease exists and is a pandemic that may stand the test of time for a while before its elimination. The truth and the fact still remain that as for now, there is no approved permanent medication or prescription that can efficiently combat the coronavirus, and the best treatment one could offer to oneself is keeping the precautionary measures outlined by WHO and the government, which includes; regular washing of hands, use of hand sanitizers, maintaining physical distance up to one-feet apart.

However, the vaccinations in most of these strategic places in the USA has greatly reduced the number of cases and hospitalizations to manageable levels.

Most importantly, we should be wise enough to stop the spread of fake news concerning COVID-19 and linking everything to religious misconception; nonetheless, Vaccines have been proposed and not yet proved to be efficacious. Note also, "prevention is better than cure, and a healthy man is a wealthy man."

www.ingramcontent.com/pod-product-compliance
Lightning Source LLC
Chambersburg PA
CBHW031417210526
45464CB00005B/1928